Philanthropos

Physiological Cruelty

Fact v. fancy - an inquiry into the vivisection question

Philanthropos

Physiological Cruelty
Fact v. fancy - an inquiry into the vivisection question

ISBN/EAN: 9783337255886

Printed in Europe, USA, Canada, Australia, Japan

Cover: Foto ©Thomas Meinert / pixelio.de

More available books at **www.hansebooks.com**

PHYSIOLOGICAL CRUELTY:

OR,

FACT *v.* FANCY.

AN INQUIRY INTO THE VIVISECTION QUESTION.

BY

PHILANTHROPOS.

LONDON:
TINSLEY BROS., 8, CATHERINE STREET, STRAND.
1883.

PREFACE.

IN compiling this little book, my aim has been to place in the hands both of professional and unprofessional readers a short compendium of the principal established facts and most obvious reasonings on the question of Experiment upon Living Animals. I venture to hope that such a work may prove useful to medical men who have not time to consult books of reference, and examine into the details of the subject for themselves, without its being too technical to interest those of the general public who are willing to give thought and attention to a most important matter. I must risk the accusation of being either too professional, or too popular, only pleading that I have, at any rate, endeavoured to avoid inaccuracy.

London, April, 1883.

TABLE OF CONTENTS.

CHAPTER I.—INTRODUCTORY.
PAGE
Duty of unprejudiced Investigation—Object of this Book . . 1

CHAPTER II.—WHAT IS PAIN?
Our knowledge of Pain derived from human experience alone—The process of Sensation and Pain—Reflex action independent of consciousness—Vagueness of "signs of Pain"—Definition of Pain—Feeling and Irritability—Feeling dependent on consciousness—Its relation to mental development—Animals less sensitive than Men—Mental element of Pain—Absence of this in animals —Examples—Amount of Pain in operations—Painlessness of Convalescence—Insensitiveness of brain substance—Example . 4

CHAPTER III.—WHAT IS CRUELTY?
Cruelty defined—What is sufficient justification for giving Pain? —Not merely the good of the sufferer—Nor his consent—But the attainment of an adequate benefit—Benefits aimed at in Physiological Experiment—These surpass the evil of Pain in quality—And exceed it in quantity—Consequently the benefit aimed at is adequate—Answer to objection 20

CHAPTER IV.—OUR RIGHTS OVER ANIMALS.
Experiments on animals asserted to be abstractly wrong—Reasons usually given—Experiment not necessarily demoralizing to the operator—Universality and beneficence of the Law of Vicarious Suffering—Our right to apply it to animals for our benefit— Vagueness of the principle generally acted on—The true principle—Mr. Hutton's principle—Impossibility of carrying it out —Summary 31

CHAPTER V.—WHAT IS VIVISECTION?
What is Vivisection?—Various definitions — Dissecting alive— True sense of the word—Course of study in physiological laboratories—Histological department—Chemical department—Physical department—Experiments upon detached tissue and organs —Experiments upon pithed animals—Painful experiments—Inoculations—Testing of drugs—Use of anæsthetics—Statistics of experiments performed—Conclusion 40

CHAPTER VI.—THE RELATION OF EXPERIMENT TO PHYSIOLOGY.
Many non-physiological systems—Only one physiological system —The Empirical system—The Physiological system founded on Experiment—Experiment on living animals part of a rational method of investigation—The Circulation of the Blood—Blood pressure—Contractile power of the arteries—The Absorbent

PAGE

Vessels—Discoveries of Aselli and Pecquet—Value of this knowledge—Respiration—Changes effected in the inspired air —Changes effected in the blood—Digestion—The Nervous System—Discoveries of Bell, Magendie, and others—Present state of our knowledge on the subject—Muscular action— Discoveries of Haller—Summary 51

CHAPTER VII.—THE RELATION OF MEDICINE TO EXPERIMENT.
The subject a complicated one—An amputation in old times—An amputation at the present day—Facial nerves—Artificial respiration—Transfusion of blood—Orthopædic surgery—Internal operations—Chassaignac's *écraseur*—Removal of one kidney —Removal of larynx—"Animal grafting"—Study of the processes of disease—Testing of drugs—Preventive medicine— Other benefits of experiment 68

CHAPTER VIII.—LEGISLATION : PAST, PRESENT, AND POSSIBLE.
General state of the law—Martin's Act—No English physiologist prosecuted under it—The "Hand-book to the Physiological Laboratory"—The Norwich experiment—Appointment of the Royal Commission—Its conclusions from the evidence—Recommendations—The Act of 1876—Its principal provisions—Defects—Autocracy of the Home Secretary—Mode of proceeding under the Act—Action of the Home Secretary—Bill for the Total Abolition of Vivisection—Desirable modifications in the working of the Act—Responsibility to be left to the signatories—Certificates unnecessary for inoculations—Licenses held by medical instructors to hold good for their term of office— What is abstractly desirable 83

CHAPTER IX.—CONCLUSION.
Summary of previous argument—Supposed demoralization of experimenters—Where the real danger lies—Conclusion . . 103

APPENDIX.

APPENDIX A.—POPULAR FALLACIES ABOUT EXPERIMENT . . 112
APPENDIX B.—AMOUNT OF SUFFERING INFLICTED . . . 119
APPENDIX C.—NECESSITY OF EXPERIMENTAL RESEARCH, FOR THE WELFARE OF MAN AND OF THE LOWER ANIMALS.
Section I. Utility to Man.—Section II. Utility to Animals . . 129
APPENDIX D.—THE FUNDAMENTAL DISCOVERIES DUE TO EXPERIMENT UPON LIVING ANIMALS.
Harvey and the circulation of the Blood—Discovery of the Lacteals 136
APPENDIX E.—THE MEDICAL MINORITY.
Evidence given before the Royal Commission—Subsequent Literature 142
APPENDIX F.—LEGISLATION.
Object of Legislation recommended by Royal Commission—Scope of Legislation recommended by Royal Commission—Manner in which the Act is administered 152

PHYSIOLOGICAL CRUELTY.

CHAPTER I.

INTRODUCTORY.

Duty of unprejudiced Investigation.—Object of this Book.

WHEN a question has been made the subject of hot debate, and been tossed up and down in discussions where feeling has played as large a part as argument, it becomes enveloped in a dust-cloud of words, sweeping charges, and irrelevant recriminations, in which it is difficult to keep sight of the central object. The first duty, then, of any one who wishes to see the truth for himself, and to show it to others, is to get rid, as far as may be, of all this turmoil,—at least, to keep the door of his own mind close shut against it,—to silence any strong prepossessions for one side or the other, and strive quietly to see the thing which *is*, not that which he hopes, or fears, or thinks may be.

This is never an easy thing to do; and in the "Vivisection" controversy it is peculiarly difficult, for it involves the sacrifice on both sides of the strongest feeling involved. A physiologist must lay aside his abstract devotion to Science; he can no longer use the advancement of her interests as the ready test of his work, and the sanction of her greatest servants as his justification; but he must be content to inquire whether the practice of performing experiments on living animals is or is not reconcileable with true humanity, and what is its effect upon the moral sense of those who use or approve it. On the other hand, a lay man or woman must not be swayed by the natural love of animals, and dislike to the infliction of pain, which make it grievous to think that any feeling creature has been hurt deliberately; still less must they excite their feelings by the attempt to realize the necessarily repugnant details of the operations, and to imagine their own pet dogs subjected to them. What they have to ascertain is—what is really done of this sort, whether what is done is necessary, whether it is justifiable, and how it is regarded by those who practise it. The question of whether it is pleasant or painful to think of has absolutely no more to do with the matter than it has with surgical operations, which few of the general public would care to witness, or to hear described in detail. I do not write for readers who take a pleasure in ghastly descriptions and ugly minutiæ, which are totally unnecessary for the discussion of principles. Such a pleasure is morbid, and I desire to address only the sane. That class of mind which, in a lower stratum of society, revels in the *Police News* and the "penny dreadfuls," will never be at a loss to provide itself with repulsive literature, and I shall not cater for it. In the text of this little book, therefore, there will be found only such medical details as are indispensable to the argument, further information on special points being added in the Appendix.

I desire now to make an attempt to look fairly at all the points of this large subject, and to carry my readers step by step along the inquiry which has brought my own mind to certain definite conclusions. We shall insist, as we go along, upon knowing exactly what we mean and are discussing, and having a clear idea for every word used. We shall endeavour to trace the moral principles which bear upon the matter, and to learn how to apply them. We shall examine into the actual relations of Physiology and Medicine to Experiment in the past, and thence deduce their probable relation in the future. We shall see what is and has been the state of affairs in England as to experiment upon living animals in our own day, both before and after the passing of the "Cruelty to Animals Act," of 1876, —what has been done in the laboratories, what is permitted by the law. Thence we shall be able to conclude whether any changes are desirable in the nature or administration of the law; and if so, what they should be.

There has been enough, and too much, of personal controversy over the "Vivisection" question, and I would rather avoid adding to it. As far as possible, it seems best to consider the absolute facts and reasons which bear on the subject, and draw our own conclusions, without stopping by the way to argue with every one who has arrived at a different result; but in reaching any conclusions at all, one is obliged to differ from thinkers either of such eminence or of such influence that to take no notice of their arguments would seem arrogant or cowardly. It will, therefore, be necessary to discuss some of the most notable statements and arguments which have appeared in print.

As far as possible, I shall give references and authorities for every assertion of fact which can be disputed by any one with a reasonable knowledge of the subject; and I ask from my readers only that candid attention, and that openness of mind, which are the absolute conditions of finding truth in any direction whatever.

The point chiefly in dispute is the rightfulness of giving pain to animals for certain purposes; consequently, the question which meets us at the outset of our enquiry is— What *is* pain?

CHAPTER II.

WHAT IS PAIN?

Our knowledge of Pain derived from human experience alone—The process of Sensation and Pain—Reflex action independent of Consciousness—Vagueness of "signs of Pain"—Definition of Pain—Feeling and Irritability—Feeling dependent on consciousness—Its relation to mental development—Animals less sensitive than men—Mental element of Pain—Absence of this in animals—Examples—Amount of Pain in operations—Painlessness of convalescence—Insensitiveness of brain substance—Example.

ALL that we know about Pain is derived from human experience. This seems very obvious, but not the less it is often forgotten. As a matter of fact, we *know* nothing about any pain except what we have ourselves suffered. We cannot feel with another person's nerves: and when he describes his feelings, we cannot be sure that the words he uses bear the same meaning to him as they do to us: but we take for granted a general analogy between him and ourselves, based on our common nature; and from time to time we correct this assumption, as we discover minor differences between us, and conclude perhaps that he feels pain more or less acutely than we do. As men have been acting on this assumption for centuries, and constantly comparing experiences, there has grown up an average standard of human sensibility, by which we guide ourselves, and which allows us to say in a rough way that such and such a person is insensitive or hypersensitive.

But when we have to do with animals, we lose ourselves at once. The community of nature from which we argued with men, has sunk from an identity of species to a similarity of type; the comparison of experiences by which we corrected our conclusions, is impossible. We have nothing left to guide us except an analogy with ourselves which we know must be misleading, and "signs of pain," which are of all indications the vaguest. They are thus vague, because all that they prove is that something is going on which the organism repels; but they do not prove that there is any consciousness of it, and if there is consciousness they do not show the degree of feeling. This will be clearer if we glance at what actually happens when an injury of any kind is inflicted.

Every one knows that there are two great classes of nerves,—the *afferent*, which convey messages (or, more properly, impulses) to the brain and spinal cord,—and the *efferent*, which bring away impulses from it. The afferent nerves alone can convey those impulses which give rise to feeling; the efferent nerves are quite incapable of doing so, and their chief business is to convey those impulses which excite motion. The afferent nerves mainly begin in small organs called touch-corpuscles, great numbers of which are situated in the skin, making it much more sensitive than the deeper tissues. If you drop some hot sealing-wax on a person's hand, all the little terminals of the spot on which it falls are suddenly stimulated, and there is an instant change in the activity of their molecules. Then a change runs along the nerve-fibre to which they belong, until it reaches the spinal cord, where it enters a ganglion, or knot of nerve-cells, full of independent energy. A portion of the impulse will be communicated to the fibres which go up to the brain; while some of the energy latent in the ganglion will be released by the arriving shock, run down an efferent nerve, and set in motion the muscles of the hand and arm,—and the hand will be pulled away. This process sounds long in describing, but we feel it to be done instantaneously. It can be carried out by the nerves and the ganglion, quite independently of that part of the impulse which went on to the brain,—and what becomes of that need not necessarily affect the action. Its fate will depend upon the condition in which it finds the brain. That organ may be awake and ready to attend to it, and in that case there will be a keen feeling of pain; it may be absorbed in its own work, carrying on thought, and give it only a half attention,—and then (especially if the stimulus has not been of quite so strong a kind as the one supposed) there will be a faint impression made on the mind, and soon forgotten; or it may be stupefied by narcotics, and take no notice at all, and in that case there will, of course, be no feeling of pain whatever. But whether pain be keenly felt, or faintly, or not at all,—the jerk away of the hand, which is the outward sign of pain, will be present all the same, unless the narcotizing has been so performed as to affect the nerve-centres in the spinal marrow which govern reflex actions, as well as the brain. So long as only the higher centres are laid asleep, reflex actions will go on, even more markedly and with greater energy than when it is awake. People operated upon under chloroform will shrink and scream, because the stimulus from the irritated nerves has gone round to the nervous centres which set the vocal organs in motion; but their intellectual and higher sensory centres are asleep, and they feel nothing. It will not do to say that they did feel the pain at the time, but have forgotten it; for, firstly, they will sometimes remember having heard themselves scream; and, if so, why should they not remember the much stronger impression of pain? and, secondly, when they are only partially narcotized, they feel some pain, and remember that they have done so,—whence it is only reasonable to conclude that when they remember no pain it is because they have felt none. Therefore, even cries do not prove that pain is really felt, because they do not prove that the brain is in a condition to feel it. It is the same with motions, jerks, or struggles. We have seen that the process which makes us jerk away our hand, for instance, from any painful touch, can go on quite independently of consciousness. It may go on where we *know* that there is no consciousness. If a person's neck or back is broken (*i.e.*, if the spinal marrow is so severed or injured that impulses can no longer pass the place of the injury), there will be no consciousness of what goes on below it. Such a person's foot might be cut off, and he would never feel it. Prick the leg, he will tell you that he has no sensation of pain, yet the leg will be pulled away from the prick; tickle the sole of his foot, and the foot will be jerked away. What is more, such reflex actions will be much more violent than they would have been if he had been conscious, probably because all the energy of the impulse is expended upon producing motion, and none of it upon producing sensation. It is often difficult to keep such patients covered up in bed, because the slightest tickling or irritation from the bedclothes will make them kick them off. A horse can kick after he is dead. A knacker, after he has cut off a horse's head, will pass a long rod down the spinal marrow to destroy its activity; otherwise, as soon as he began to skin the body, the legs would kick with sufficient force to break his arm.* Such a motion in response to a stimulation is called

* Evidence of Dr. Anthony before the Royal Commission on Vivisection, Q. 2484.

in scientific language a *reaction*; in agitationist language it is called a "spasm of agony."* It is best marked where there is no agony at all, which is, perhaps, a reason for preferring the former phrase. Motions, cries, jerks, and struggles cannot, therefore, be depended upon as indications of pain.

But it may be asked; If so, why do physiologists performing experiments under anæsthetics tell us that they give a fresh dose whenever they see the animal move? Clearly, in order to be a long way on the safe side. When the reflex functions of the spinal cord are laid at rest, the consequent anæsthesia is deeper than when only the higher brain centres are affected; and we have the test of motion for the one, and have no test for the other. It is known that an animal *may be* unconscious while it struggles vehemently; but there is no doubt that it *is* unconscious, when it does not struggle at all; and to save it pain and keep it quiet for the time are the objects of the operator; he need not also think constantly of the danger of its succumbing to the anæsthetic, as he would with a human subject,—consequently, he gives it much more freely.

It would of course be absurd to say that there are no such things as signs of pain; all that can be said is that such indications are exceedingly vague, and cannot be interpreted rightly without a knowledge of the condition of the brain. When we see a creature struggling and kicking, or hear it cry, we cannot tell from that alone whether it is feeling pain, or whether it is feeling much or little. In order to know if it feels *any* pain, we must know whether its consciousness is at work, or whether the impulse is circling round its nerves and muscles, without

---

* "The very fact that physiologists select delicate petted dogs to exhibit reactions (*anglicé*, spasms of agony) under their operations . ." Miss Cobbe, in *Fortnightly Review*, January, 1882.

arousing the brain at all; and in order to know if it feels *much* pain, we must know what sort of cognizance its brain is capable of taking of such messages, when they do arouse it. In other words: In order to judge of the pain suffered by any creature (human or other), we must be acquainted with both the ordinary quality and the present condition of its brain.

Pain (like many other words upon which much depends) is used with a good deal of ambiguity. It is often far from clear—even to the speaker—whether he means by it the effect produced upon the nerves or upon the organism, whether he is thinking of what the nerves feel or of what the creature feels. Yet there is a deep distinction. One often hears it said that a person has undergone a very painful operation, but that he did not feel it, because he was under chloroform. As soon as we look at this critically, we are inclined to ask: If he could not feel, he could have no pain; and if he had no pain, how was the operation painful? And the criticism seems valid. There is evidently a confusion between two meanings of the same word, and confused speaking leads to confused thinking. Let us therefore avoid both, by clearly defining the sense in which we use our terms.

A moderate stimulation of a nerve produces an agreeable or a useful effect. Nerves were meant to work, and for each there is a degree of activity which is normal and pleasant. Beyond this point stimulation becomes distressing and injurious, and, with sensory nerves, passes into pain. Pain may therefore be described as the result of *the excessive stimulation of a nerve*. Of course, if the brain is narcotized, it is not affected by this excessive stimulation (though it takes place just the same); and therefore it is not nonsense to talk of a painful operation being performed without pain. But when the brain is awake, and working healthily, it takes note of the excessive stimulation; we become conscious of it, and the result is Feeling. The *nerve*, however, is not narcotized, and then the impulse runs along it, and is reflected by the ganglion cells into the corresponding efferent nerve, which responds accordingly. This capability on the part of a nerve of being affected by stimuli—is called Irritability; it lies quite apart from consciousness, and is entirely different from Feeling. A muscle cut out of a freshly-killed animal has Irritability, because it will contract under a current of electricity; so has the heart taken from a decapitated frog, because it continues to beat, and its action can be hastened or retarded by heat, cold, or drugs; but they have no brain, and so can have no consciousness and no Feeling. So, when the cerebral hemispheres are removed from a frog, all its nerves possess their old Irritability, and the reflex actions go on as well as if it were a complete creature. Touch it, and it will jump; put a drop of acid on one leg, and it will rub it off with the other; put food into its mouth, and it will swallow; but all this time it has no Feeling, for it has no organ of consciousness, and acts like a machine, which merely moves when you work the springs. If, instead of removing the cerebral hemispheres, we suspend their action by narcotics, the effect for the time being is as if they were not there, and there may be the highest Irritability of the nerves, but still no Feeling in the creature. There may be all the signs of pain, which result from the general sensitiveness of the nervous system; but these prove that it is sensitive, and nothing more; they prove nothing about Feeling, of which we know them to be quite independent. And observe, when it is said that a pithed frog (*i.e.*, one whose spinal marrow has been cut through, near its junction with the brain), a pigeon without cerebral hemispheres, or a chloroformed cat, cannot feel, the statement is not a conjecture. We are on firm ground, because we are going upon human experience, assisted by trustworthy analogy. We have the evidence of men and women who can be questioned, and can tell us what they have felt, and not felt. We know that we cannot feel without our brains; and we find that wherever we can test the functions of the brains of other animals, they are like ours in kind, though differing in degree. We see also that the general type of the nervous system is the same in all vertebrate animals; and that its increasing specialisation, as we ascend in the scale, is all in the direction of resemblance to our own. We have, therefore, every reason to believe that the brain is always the organ of consciousness, and that when it is absent, or inactive, there can be no consciousness, and consequently no feeling.

As the existence of feeling depends upon the activity of the brain, there is a fair presumption beforehand that it also increases with the more perfect development of that organ; and we should naturally expect to find that animals can both enjoy and suffer more, as they stand higher upon the ladder of being, and that man—the highest of animals—is also chief in sensibility. We can never get inside the consciousness of a creature with which we cannot communicate; but in the human race we find a certain rough proportion between sensibility and intellectual development, which leads us to believe in a similar proportion existing in the ranks below us. Savages will undergo with equanimity tortures which no civilized man (except perhaps under great excitement) could endure; and it is impossible to believe that the prolonged pain of tattooing could be borne for the sake of ornament by any one who felt it as we should do. The arguments used for the special protection of cats and dogs against experiment are founded on this greater sensitiveness in the more highly organized creature.

There are two factors in nervous and intellectual activity. One is the structural factor, *i.e.* the actual amount of nervous matter to be set in action, the quantities of blood supplied to it, and the arrangements by which the blood bathes numerous surfaces of the brain; the other is the functional factor, *i.e.* the amount of nerve force in action, or the energy both actual and potential evolved by and stored up in the nervous cells. Neither the size of the skull, nor even the weight of the brain, is a clear index to a man's intellectual faculties, because the more ethereal component always escapes from our weights and measures. But it is clear that sensibility must vary as this supply of nervous force varies, because the same properties which cause us to think a thought enable us also to feel a sensation. If the nervous system is not easily excitable, a painful stimulus will travel through it slowly, and even while producing its appropriate reflex action, will have little power left to affect the brain, and will produce a feeble effect when it arrives there; whereas, sensitive nerves will convey impressions rapidly to a sensitive brain, and the result is a quick and vivid sensation of pain.

This all seems so obvious as to be hardly worth saying; yet it is ignored by those who argue from our feelings to those of the lower creatures, as if they were the same, and assert that animals are as sensitive as man. Their *reactions* may be as prompt as those of men, *because a larger proportion of their nervous energy works through the spinal cord and inferior brain-centres, and less is expended on thought.* But the question is not—Does a prick of a needle make them start as quickly as a man would? but—What impression does this needle-prick make on their consciousness? And the answer must depend upon the amount of nervous energy which goes to vivify that consciousness. But the very fact that man's intellectual activity is so much greater shows that a larger surplus vitalizes his brain, and proves that the whole stock of nervous energy from which that surplus is taken must be larger than that of inferior creatures. Therefore, though an animal's nerves may display as much *irritability* as a man's, it is impossible that it can have as much *feeling* as he has, for the simple reason that it has not as much stuff to make them both out of. In fact, seeing that its mental power (which is the index of its supply of nervous force) is so much less than his, we should be more inclined to believe that its actual feeling came near his feeling, if the demonstration of it were less; because (as was said before) we see that in human beings reflex actions are most marked when there is no intellectual action, *i.e.*, when they are asleep, narcotized, or have sustained injury of the spinal cord.

Thus much about the raw material (so to speak) of pain,— the nerves which convey the impulse to the brain, and the brain which receives it. But there is a distinct element contributed to the feeling of pain by this organ itself, actively as well as passively. In all that adult human beings suffer there is a mental factor which is almost absent in animals. It cannot be better described than in the words of Mr. Edmund Gurney. " The sense of rebellion, the helpless beating about of the intellect, the counting of time, and vivid sense that each moment will be like the last, the demand ever urgent and ever baffled to find a meaning for such experience,—more than all, the sense of wrong that comes from comparison, the consciousness of self as an *exception*, of clueless isolation, of being marked off from normal sentient life by an intolerable something which none can share,—all this points to the close relation of suffering to intelligence; and the consequent difference between man and brute would presumably be at its maximum in cases of protracted suffering *below* the agony-point where intellect is too blinded to be active."*

Such intelligent creatures as dogs have, of course, memory, and are capable of recalling places and things which have been associated with suffering, and disliking them; but with an average dog such memory is faint, as compared with what we should exert under the circumstances. Dogs kept at physiological laboratories for the purpose of experiments (of course, not severe ones, as animals cannot ever be kept alive to undergo these again and again,) display no such horror of the operating room as was described in a sensational paragraph (without names or authentication) which was sent the round of the papers some time ago. A dog released from experiment has been known to jump up upon the operating table and sit there to inspect with interest his companion having his turn, showing that no very painful impression could have been left on his mind by whatever disagreeables he had undergone. Dogs with gastric fistulæ (*i.e.*, with an opening in the stomach, in which a silver tube is usually fixed,) enjoy life in perfect health, and will sit up or lie down when told, to have different substances injected or extracted. At Professor Ludwig's laboratory, in Leipzig, the dogs used as subjects for many such experiments are neither tied nor chloroformed, but merely patted and talked to while the process is going on.

Among human creatures we see the effect of mental development upon the sense of pain very clearly in the case of children. An infant can be vaccinated without making it cry, if its mind is kept occupied by a bit of sugar

* "A Chapter in the Ethics of Pain," *Fortnightly Review*, December, 1881.

held before it; and it will undergo even much more pain without discomposure, if well amused. But when that child is three or four years older, he will understand that something is going to be done to him; he will be terrified at the preparations; neither sugar nor anything else will divert his mind; and he will be conscious of all the pain given, and probably exaggerate it from terror. If pain can thus be a secondary thought in the minds of infants, it can be still more so in that of animals.

A house-dog met with an accident, by which a large piece of the skin and flesh above the eyebrow was cut, and hung loose over the eye. His master, a surgeon (who furnishes the anecdote), determined to stitch it. Now, it is well known that—the skin being extremely sensitive—stitching is one of the most painful parts even of serious operations. The dog was taken into a shed, muzzled—for the safety of the operator—and the cut stitched up. All the time that it was being done, he was straining and struggling to get away, though never whining nor crying. The instant he was released, he dashed into a corner of the shed, and seized a bone which he had had his eye upon, and which had possessed his soul while he had been undergoing operation without anæsthetics, and proceeded to enjoy it.

A horse, whose leg was badly broken, was sentenced to be shot, but there was considerable delay before the execution could take place. The bones were completely broken through, so that the leg hung loose, a state of things during which the least motion causes a human patient most exquisite agony. No suffering is worse than that from a broken bone, and the only way to prevent its becoming intolerable is to avoid the slightest jar which can grate the fragments against each other or the surrounding flesh. But during the two hours between its injury and its death this horse grazed, *and limped about to graze,* carrying the fractured limb dangling !*

Such cases as these leave it no longer to conjecture whether animals feel as keenly as we do. We knew beforehand that they were not likely to do so, on account of their lower mental calibre, implying an inferior supply of nervous energy, and also on account of the absence of the mental element in their sufferings; we saw that their *reactions* (commonly called "signs of pain") proved only irritability, and not feeling; and here is absolute demonstration of the truth of our inferences.

It may be well to add a few words on the absolute painfulness of important operations, both upon the human subject and upon animals, whether for purposes of cure or of experiment. The suffering is really much exaggerated. The cutting of the skin is very painful, because it is amply provided with fine twigs of nerves, and, above all, with the terminals of nerves. But the deeper tissues below are, for the most part, only sparsely penetrated by trunks of nerves, and are supplied with nerve terminals which have nothing to do with sensation; and unless a nerve trunk be cut (when there is a momentary flash of intense pain), there is little feeling. From the few operations that must still be done without the use of anæsthetics, surgeons know that only the cutting of the skin causes the patients any great degree of pain. Indeed, the deeper structures may be probed, incised, or pinched, without causing even uneasiness, except a nerve-fibre lie in the way of the instrument. In such a case, the patient being a man, we can hear what is really felt, and know that the pain is moderate, even with

---

* Both this and the preceding anecdote are vouched for by eye-witnesses, and will doubtless recall to most readers similar instances of the indifference shown by even the most sensitive of our domestic animals to what we should call intense pain.

extensive laceration of the deeper soft parts. Such facts show us that it is not safe to judge of what is terrible to suffer by what is terrible to witness.

The pain of convalescence is often counted among the sufferings inflicted upon animals by experiment, and not obviated by chloroform. But in reality they scarcely suffer at all. It cannot be supposed that they are worse off than human beings recovering from severe operations, and as long as no complications set in, such patients are easy and comfortable. Even a severe cutting operation which removes some source of irritation, is felt to give immediate relief; the mere healing of the cut surfaces actually causes no pain; and if one questions the recent "operation cases" in the surgical ward of a hospital as to how they feel, the usual answer is "quite comfortable." Indeed, if it is not, the surgeon suspects that something has gone wrong, and the wound must be examined. The healthy flesh of animals heals more rapidly and even more painlessly than that of men, and their supposed sufferings during convalescence are really a myth.

The introduction of the *aseptic** treatment of wounds has certainly assisted to ensure this complete absence of pain after cutting operations. As inflammation is thus warded off, the heat, swelling, and painful throbbing, which are almost inseparable from its slightest form, are also prevented. Some time ago, a case was brought into a police-court, in which a surgeon was charged with having kept monkeys in torture for months, because he had performed a series of experiments upon their brains. Now, what were the facts? During the whole of the actual operation, it was necessary to keep the animals in a state of profound anæsthesia; the most exquisite care was needed

* Treatment with carbolic acid, in order to destroy the microscopic organisms which cause inflammation in wounds.

in its performance, that the result might be successful; the wounds were treated antiseptically, to avoid inflammation, and as a result, it only took place in one case out of the twenty-six operated upon. How then were these animals "tortured"?

It seems to be supposed by many people who write on this subject, that injuries to the brain are in themselves painful; and the ugly expressions "washing the brain away" and "reducing a dog's brain to the condition of a lately-hoed potato-field"* are quoted and re-quoted as if they implied the infliction of horrors. But as a matter of fact, injury to the brain itself causes *no* pain, and wounds of the skull often pass through their entire course without the patient having even a headache. The accurate scientific account of such an injury, occurring in a human being, which appears in a recent German medical periodical, seems to put the question beyond doubt. A youth, aged 18, received a blow of a hammer in the temple, which cut the scalp, fractured the skull, and ruptured the covering of the brain. The result of this was that a considerable quantity of the brain-substance escaped on three several days. The wound was dressed aseptically, and healed shortly without any inflammation. Although many paralytic symptoms followed, the patient never lost consciousness, and remembered perfectly every circumstance connected with the injury, symptoms, and treatment, from first to last. From the time when the wound was first dressed, to its complete healing and the disappearance of all symptoms, *he never complained of any pain, nor even had the least headache.*† Every practical surgeon is familiar with cases proving equally well the want of sensibility in the substance of the brain.

* Miss Cobbe, quoting from a German writer.
† "Ein Fall Traumatischer Aphasie." Sitzungsbericht der Würzburg. Phys. Med. Gesellschaft, 1882.

Such cases enable us to estimate the value of the indignation expended upon all these experiments on the brain. The only pain given is that to the feelings of tender-hearted people ignorant of physiology; but that appears to have been so intense as to render it necessary to stop the experiments, arrest English inquiry into the functions of the brain, and limit the gaining of experience in the treatment of its injuries to what can be acquired by Nature's experiments upon human subjects.

We have now seen that the Feeling of Pain is dependent upon Consciousness, and, in a certain degree, proportionate to Intellect; consequently, an animal at any time suffers less than a man would do from the same cause; and under anæsthetics (like man) does not suffer at all. Injuries to the brain are painless to men, and must, therefore, be painless to animals. Prolonged and deep operations are not more painful to men than superficial ones (since the cutting of the skin is the acutely painful phase of any operation), and therefore they cannot be so to animals; and we have moreover seen from facts, that what would cause us agony hardly disturbs their equanimity. Convalescence after operations is normally painless to both. All these facts must be borne in mind in further discussing the question of experiment on Living Animals.

CHAPTER III.

WHAT IS CRUELTY?

Cruelty defined—What is sufficient justification for giving Pain?—Not merely the good of the sufferer—Nor his consent—But the attainment of an adequate benefit—Benefits aimed at in Physiological Experiment—These surpass the evil of Pain in quality—And exceed it in quantity—Consequently the benefit aimed at is adequate—Answer to objection.

We are all agreed that cruelty is wrong.

The question to be solved, therefore, is:—*What is cruelty?*

The simplest thorough definition seems to be:—*The wanton or excessive infliction of pain.*

The *wanton* infliction of pain is that for which there is no justification; the *excessive* is that for which there is justification in fact, but not in degree. Both terms imply that there can be such justification. Let us try to ascertain what it is.

The first consideration that suggests itself is—that it is justifiable to inflict pain upon another for its own good. We act upon this principle constantly, with clear consciences, and in the cases of those whom we love best. In the education of children, and the care of the sick, or in the treatment of criminals—who are socially children, and morally sick—we do not hesitate to refuse what is pleasant, and enforce what is painful. But this principle is not a sufficient guide. It is quite possible to do something which is really cruel, for the good of the sufferer. Let us suppose a case. Two children—a boy and a girl—are disfigured by teeth which have been allowed to grow crooked. The mischief has gone so far that it can only be remedied by long and painful treatment. There will be constant discomfort and distress for months, and tooth drawing and other very painful minor operations from time to time. The teeth are sound, and there is no danger of worse consequences than the ugly appearance. It is certainly for the children's good that this should be amended, and the father takes them to a dentist. But the boy is very nervous and sensitive; he suffers agonies of terror at the mere rattle of the instruments in the drawer; he is reduced to fainting by his first experience of them, and loses his sleep from pain and general nervous misery. Would not any friend advise the father:—" Give it up; it is cruelty to torment the child so for a matter of mere appearance; when he is grown up he can wear a moustache and partly hide the defect; and, after all, looks are of little consequence to a man"? Whereas, if the boy were sturdy and robust, his father would do well to encourage him to bear the pain, or even insist on his doing so, for his future advantage. But with the girl he would be much more unwilling to give up the attempt, and his lady friends would certainly urge him to persevere, reminding him that if her health suffered from pain and fright, she might be nursed up into strength afterwards; but that there would never be another chance of saving her from disfigurement, and it would be a serious drawback to her through life. In this case, the pain is always inflicted for the good of the individual, whether girl or boy; but our judgment of whether its infliction is cruel or not, varies according to the proportion between the pain given and the object aimed at. Hence we conclude that—Pain given for the good of the individual itself may be unjustifiable, *if the good to be obtained is not sufficient.*

Another qualification which naturally occurs to the mind is the consent of the sufferer. It may be urged that there can be no cruelty with the goodwill of the person chiefly concerned. But in the case which we have just been considering, if the boy had been very conscientious and obedient, as well as very nervous and sensitive, it would surely have increased the father's cruelty, if he had used the child's conscience to enforce unreasonably harsh commands. Let us suppose another case, this time of suffering with consent for the good of others. It is said that the wife of an American doctor allowed herself to be inoculated with a decoction of mouldy straw, in order to see if the result would be an attack of measles, which proved to be the case. Measles (though extremely unpleasant) is not a very painful complaint; and when we think of the risk that the lady ran, and of the discomfort to which she submitted, in order to further her husband's investigations, we are only inclined to admire her devotion to him and to science. But suppose that his ascendancy over her mind had induced her to let him inoculate her with leprosy, in order to try the agonizing modes of cure in use among the natives of some of the South Sea Islands. Should we not feel that he had been guilty of cruelty, and that obtaining her consent was no palliation? Suppose, besides, that he had no intention of practising on leprous cases, or of publishing his results, but was merely gratifying a scientific curiosity; would he not be deemed brutal beyond excuse? On the other hand, suppose that he had nearly perfected a mode of healing, however painful, and needed but one test case to decide some critical point; after which he intended to devote his life to curing what had been hitherto held to be incurable. If, now, his wife gives herself up to the experiment, and he carries it out, do we not feel that the case is altered? We may blame it as the very madness of sacrifice, or we may honour it as the sublime of self-devotion, but it is no longer a question of cruelty. Here again, the consent of the sufferer is always present; but whether the pain be supposed the same, or greatly intensified, we judge the total action according to the benefit aimed at; and conclude that—Pain given with the consent of the individual is unjustifiable, *if the good to be obtained is not sufficient.*

We are thus constantly thrown back—for a test of the justifiable infliction of pain—upon a certain proportion existing between the evil of suffering caused and the benefit of whatever kind sought to be obtained. In a general way, we can roughly estimate this for ourselves, and do. Every one, sooner or later, has to give pain, or to be the cause of its being given; and this comparative estimate is either deliberately worked out,—or half-consciously made in the back of his mind, by old-established habits of judging, —or brutally and carelessly neglected. Upon whether he makes it or not, depends the question of his personal cruelty. Any one who hurts another sentient creature without intending to obtain a good greater than the harm that he does, is in so far cruel. He may be mistaken in his calculations, and obtain no good at all; and then his act has proved a cruel one, but he himself was not so. This is the justification of the sportsman. If he defends his sport to his own conscience, he does it by weighing the gain to himself and others in strength, health, skill, and daring, against the sufferings of the game, which he tries to make as slight as possible. If he is convinced that the advantages preponderate, he pursues his amusement with a clear conscience, and is not cruel; but if we did not agree with his estimate we should pronounce the sport cruel, and wonder that a humane man did not see it to be so. On the other hand, if he took no heed of the pain which he gave, did not try to reduce it as low as possible, or feel that it needed to be justified, we should then condemn him as brutal; and, much more, if he took any pleasure in looking on at these sufferings.

What is true of the sportsman is equally true of the scientific experimenter. If a physiologist gives pain without being convinced that the object he has in view justifies it, if he is indifferent as to its amount, neglectful of alleviating or preventing it, where possible,—above all, if he takes any pleasure in witnessing it,—he is cruel; and if he is also eminent, his eminence only lifts high his fault, and mingles bars of shadow in the glory of an illustrious name. And as we have now to do with scientific experiment, we will leave aside all the other causes for which pain may be given, and enquire only: What are the benefits aimed at in such experiments, and how can they be estimated in comparison with pain, when any is given?

The widest and highest aim of physiological experiment, whether painful or painless, is the advance of physiological knowledge; and this is the one which scientific medical men regard most highly, and which it is most difficult to make laymen regard at all. Every scrap of knowledge is turned to practical account sooner or later; the sounder and more accurate that knowledge is, the more trustworthy are the conclusions drawn from it; the more doctors learn of the nature and working of the machine they have to repair, the less likely they are to make mistakes in dealing with it, and be it remembered that *a medical mistake may mean a lost life*. But this is too long an outlook for popular legislation, and under our present law, no experiment is allowed of which the beneficial object is not direct and immediate. This does not affect the line of argument; for the benefits sought are the same in both cases; only by advancing Physiology they are sought indirectly, and on a large scale, instead of directly, on a small one. They may be resumed in four: *relief from pain, lengthened life, restoration of mental or bodily activity, and restoration to health.*

How can we now bring these into comparison with pain, and find a common measure by which to estimate their values? It is not impossible. There are two modes in which a good may exceed an evil, in *quality* and in *quantity*. It may be of a higher class, or it may be of a larger amount. If it should exceed in one and be exceeded in the other, the balance would be very difficult to strike; but if it exceeded in both, the question would be solved beyond dispute. Such is the case here; and we find our common measure in *ease*, freedom from pain. Ease and pain are exact equivalents in quality; one is a good, the other is an evil, but they are both of the same order. So let A and B be two individuals of the same nature, and exactly alike. If pain be inflicted upon A by which B is relieved from the same amount of pain, and the relief and the suffering last for the same length of time, it is evident that an exact equivalent has been obtained, but no more. But longer life is a benefit of a higher class than ease; for men will cling to life and pray for it, in spite of discomfort, and even severe pain. And mental or bodily activity are better things than ease; for men will endure pain rather than cloud their minds with opiates, and toil on when every exertion is distress, and we honour them for so doing. Health, again, includes ease, and also the capacity for those activities which we have just seen to be superior to it. Therefore:

Ease is (as to quality) equal to pain:
Long life is superior to ease;

Activity is superior to ease;
Health is superior to ease.

Conclusion: Long life, mental and bodily activity, and health, are benefits which in quality more than balance the evil of pain. And if A's pain purchases them for B, it has been fully counterbalanced.

But, it may be said, although the life of the victim may not be shortened, yet while it is being kept in pain for the sake of all these beneficial results to another, *its* activities are suspended and *its* health destroyed. This is true, and brings us a step farther. If A and B are exactly equal creatures, the loss of activity to one is not more than balanced by the gain to the other. But if B belongs to a superior class—much more, if he is a man and A is any other animal—the activities saved will be very much more varied, numerous, and efficient than those sacrificed; and the scale will again dip on the side of benefit. Of course, human activities are sometimes so perverted as to be positively injurious to society and to the man himself; but these are exceptional cases. As a rule, "a man is better than a sheep,"[*] or even than "a dog, cat, mule, ass, or horse."[†] The conclusion which cannot be escaped is—that if the keeping of one rabbit, dog, or other animal in pain could buy the health, long life, or activity of one man who would otherwise have suffered equal pain, died, or been rendered useless, a distinct advantage has been gained to the community and to the universe. We reach a stand-point in this minimum of benefit. Let any one who dislikes the conclusion answer distinctly: If the question is whether a man or a rabbit shall have a certain amount of pain, is it better that it should be the man? And if it is not better that he should have the pain, is it better that he should have what is worse to him than the pain?

[*] Matth. xii. 12.   [†] Cruelty to Animals Act, 1876.

It is now clear that the evil inflicted on animals in painful experiments is exceeded in *quality* by the good sought to be obtained for man. We have next to compare the two in *quantity*.

We have hitherto been supposing that the pain suffered lasted as long as the benefit purchased. But this is never the case. The most prolonged painful experiment that could be imagined would only last during a few hours*, a far shorter time than many an agonizing disease; but a restoration to health or a relief from pain for such a time would never be thought worth counting among the good results of experimental medicine. To cure a sick man is generally to give him a period of restored health and efficiency which may be counted by years; at any rate, whatever is worth calling "a cure" at all lasts for much longer than the longest painful experiment. The pain passes, the relief remains; the lower creature finds a speedy end to its sufferings in release or death; the man lives on in renewed health and power; what is evil is transient, what is good is enduring. Even in the case, then, of one animal suffering for one man, we see that *the good obtained exceeds the evil in quantity, because lasting longer.*

But, as a matter of fact, such a simple case of one *versus* one seldom occurs. The only instance of it is the rare one when a surgeon tries an experiment upon an animal, for the sake of perfecting himself in it, before performing it upon a man. This would seem a most righteous use of vivisection, and all the above arguments would apply to it in full force, even if the subject could not be anæsthetized. When a surgeon knows that the life or death of a fellow-creature, with all the innumerable ties of duty and affection

---

* A series of experiments might of course last longer, but then they would have intervals; and so also would an induced illness, but the animal is generally killed as soon as the disease is fully developed.

which hang round all human lives that are not desolate, is shortly to depend upon his skill, surely it is his duty to fit himself for that solemn charge by every means in his power. Besides, such experiments for gaining operative experience could nearly always be performed under chloroform; but although they might be quite painless, and their usefulness is peculiarly direct and obvious, they are expressly forbidden by our English law. We need not, therefore, consider them further.

The next simple case is that in which a definite number of animals is experimented upon for a definite object, and we know the result. For instance, we know that—in order to perfect the method of performing the operation known by his name—Mr. Spencer Wells operated upon 16 (?) anæsthetized rabbits and guinea-pigs. And we know also that with his own hand he treated successfully 600 women, who would otherwise have had an exceedingly small chance of life, considering the danger of so terrible an operation, before his experiments. We know, moreover, that this number is constantly increasing, as other surgeons of sufficient skill rise up and avail themselves of his method, while no more rabbits need be killed.

It is not often, however, that we can so distinctly put in two columns the lives sacrificed and the lives saved; and, though such instances are distinct and impressive, they are not in the least necessary to the argument. Usually experiments are made upon a number of animals which we are without means of computing;* their results are collated with and modified by other trains of investigation; and the conclusion drawn affects an unascertainable number of patients, in different degrees, qualified by the varying skill of the doctors applying it. Moreover, such experiments do not always give the expected result. Theories, which it was sought to prove by vivisection, have been disproved by

* Except in England, under the new law, of course.

it; and the result of the experiment has been to detect mistake, instead of establishing positive truth. False tracks have been started upon; and animals have bled and died, only to mark "No Thoroughfare" upon some tempting path. But though the result be negative, and the good done has been indirect, it has not been less real. Human victims would have paid the penalty of these errors, if they had not been ransomed by others of lower kind. Whether results are positive or negative, they all go to build up the fabric of an accurate and scientific physiology, upon which (as we saw before, and shall see later with more detail,) the success of medicine chiefly depends. Every patient anywhere on the globe, who is treated by any civilised doctor, profits by this sound and accurate knowledge, which owes so much—how much I shall try to show in a subsequent chapter—to experiment. And as new lives come into being, and the human race increases, the number of those who thus benefit goes on ever increasing. The consequence is that though we cannot always assign the precise share of vivisection in any investigation of which it has formed a part, yet we can always know that—whether it be great or small—*it is multiplied by a practically infinite factor.* While, if it was a painful vivisection, the pain was endured by a limited number of animals for a limited time. Thus, the greatest pain suffered for the smallest actual result would in time be fully counterbalanced, since the lowest figure, when multiplied by infinity, exceeds the largest definite sum. Much more is this the case when the result is large and visible to begin with. We conclude, therefore, that even where we have no means of knowing the number of animals which have suffered, nor the exact degree in which men have benefited by their sufferings under experiment—*the good still exceeds the evil in quantity.*

It may be objected to this argument that by it we actually destroy all proportion between the pain inflicted and the benefit expected, and would justify the most excruciating tortures, in prospect of the smallest possible addition to our knowledge. This would be true, but for two considerations. First, that in practice minute fractions must always be neglected. The very condition which saves the performance of a painful experiment from being cruelty—is the presence in the operator's mind of a distinct expectation of counterbalancing good; but if this good is diffused and attenuated over infinite time, his finite mind cannot grasp it, and the condition is clearly destroyed. Secondly, the number of individuals benefited is not really infinite, but only practically so, because incalculably large and quite indefinite. The human race must some day become extinct, and all its physical triumphs die with it. These two considerations make a *reductio ad absurdum* impossible, and leave the plain and reasonable deduction—that in order to be justified in performing a painful experiment, and free from the charge of cruelty, the operator must have in view a benefit proportional to the pain inflicted; but that the benefit need not necessarily be proved to be as great to any one individual as the pain is, because it will be shared by an indefinitely larger number, during a much longer time.

I cannot expect that the facts and arguments of the foregoing chapters will convince every one. When all has been explained and argued, there will still remain irreconcilables, determined to persist in their war against scientific experiments. But we can now see clearly what this war amounts to. It is an effort to keep many animals in suffering instead of few, men instead of beasts, the most sensitive creature instead of the less sensitive. Whereas, a true and humane physiology seeks to prevent as much as possible of human suffering, at the cost of as little as possible of animal suffering. On which side is the cruelty?

CHAPTER IV.

OUR RIGHTS OVER ANIMALS.

Experiments on animals asserted to be abstractly wrong—Reasons usually given—Experiment not necessarily demoralizing to the operator—Universality and beneficence of the Law of Vicarious Suffering—Our right to apply it to animals for our benefit—Vagueness of the principle generally acted on—The true principle—Mr. Hutton's principle—Impossibility of carrying it out—Summary.

WHEN we have proved that even painful experiments upon animals need not be cruel, we have not disposed of the whole moral difficulty; in fact, it is only then that we find ourselves face to face with the true *crux* of the question. The opponents of such experiments assert that they are wrong in themselves, and that therefore it is time wasted to prove that advantages are gained by them, since no profit can justify a crime. I most unreservedly admit that no hygienic gain is worth a moral loss, and that the health of one man's body is too dearly purchased by the disease of another man's soul. But vague declamation is not enough. It must be clearly explained to us *why* such experiments are wrong, apart from their object and result, before we can admit either to be quite immaterial considerations.

The reasons usually given are four: 1st, that they are cruel; 2nd, that the infliction of pain hardens and demoralizes the inflictor; 3rd, that it is unjust to make animals suffer for our good; 4th, that it is an infringement of their rights which we have no authority to make.

In the last chapter we saw that experiments, when performed for good reasons—are not cruel; for they are intended to save more pain than they inflict; and it cannot be cruel—of two sufferings to prefer the least.

Painful experiments—done with a serious purpose and a sufficient reason—are no more demoralizing to the performer than painful operations. In both cases there must be an absorption in the object and the process which withdraws the nerves from much of the harass of sympathy; but this is essential to the work being properly done, and has no more to do with demoralization than the hardness of a labourer's hand. It is difficult to see how the fact that the operator's object is in one case the good of his subject, and in the other the good of more numerous but remote patients, can make any difference in the effect on his morals. It may make some in the effect on his feelings, rendering the operation the easier to carry through, because the object is more immediately to be reached; but we must not confuse feelings with principles. Unsteady nerves are not the same thing as sensitive consciences; and the fact that people cannot bear to see or give pain means much more often that they are weak and selfish than that they are particularly humane.

Next comes the more serious assertion—that it is unjust to make animals suffer for our good; and as many experiments are made in investigating the diseases of animals, this spreads itself out into the general question: *Is it right that one creature should suffer for the good of another?*

Vicarious suffering is one of the darkest mysteries—as it is one of the most comprehensive laws—of the sentient world. There are times when we all rebel against its terrible and unequal pressure, and cry out passionately:

> " That not a moth with vain desire
> Be shrivelled in a fruitless fire,
> Or but subserve another's gain."

But in saner moments we bow before its stern beneficence, and recognize that it alone has moulded the forms of beauty and strength which we see around us in insect, bird, and beast; and that it alone is developing rarer and higher beauty in the spiritual life of man. The most insignificant fly that dances through a summer's day opens out its marvellous little wings with strength and dexterity, because thousands of other flies that were slow and clumsy were snapped up by their enemies; the robin pipes his autumn song, because dozens of quiet caterpillars and writhing worms have been pecked to death to feed that cheery sweetness. It is not all horror. The less goes to make the greater, the imperfect fades before the perfect, the whole creation groans and travails in pain together, yet the New Heavens and Earth are ever being born. Much more is it so in the world of men. By this law the human race is *solidaire*. The sins of the fathers are visited upon the children, and the children's sins are a curse to their fathers; but so also a blessing descends from generation to generation, and only those who stand within the shadow of the curse can lighten it. Suffering with the suffering, or for the faults and errors of other men, is the lot of all; but the knowledge of what it is so to suffer, and the certainty that our own faults and errors will lay the like on others, are among the most powerful motives to hold us back from evil. Were not our hearts bound to each other by cords which wrench one when another breaks, we should be a mass of disintegrated units, with no common life, no racial unity, lower than the beasts who do feel—if not *for*, at least, *with* each other. And this we admit and express in our worship. The apotheosis of utter self-sacrifice is that around which the Christian's most sacred thoughts and aspirations cling, which he aspires, however dimly, to imitate; at least, which he owns as the perfect ideal of manhood. And those who do not believe that that ideal ever

> "Had breath, and wrought
> With human hands the creed of creeds,"

must still confess that (tried by the most utilitarian standard) the great law of nature which secures the benefit of all by the sacrifice of some, is justified in its working.

In the abstract, then, we declare that *it is right and well that one should suffer for the sake of another*; there is nothing in it at all revolting to our moral feeling. We live by and under this law; we submit to it, because we must; we accept it, if we are wise. It is not possible to carry on this discussion with any one who rebels against it; he must become a loyal and law-abiding subject of the world he lives in, before he is qualified to discuss its administration.

The remaining question is: *Have we the right to constitute ourselves administrators of this law, and to apply it to animals for our own interest?* Nature will do so in the interest of their race if we let her alone; but when we domesticate any creature, we to a certain extent protect it from her action. We withdraw it from the struggle for existence, and substitute artificial for natural selection. We do not allow it to be starved out by stronger competitors, or devoured by wild enemies. Have we then entirely delivered it from the general law, and are we bound to make its existence nothing but a pleasurable one?

Of course no one says anything so unreasonable. It is generally admitted that we may chase and kill an animal, often necessarily with much pain, not because its life and liberty interferes with ours, but because its death will render our life more complete, perhaps in the most trivial detail. We kill them (without anæsthetics) not only that we may have food and clothing, but that the food may be varied and attractive, and the clothing rich and beautiful.* We subject them to painful mutilations in order to make them more manageable for service, to improve the flavour of their flesh, and even to please our whimsical fancies. We imprison them in cages and Zoological Gardens, to improve our knowledge of Natural History, or merely to amuse ourselves by looking at them. It is abundantly clear that in all our customary dealings with animals we apply to them without scruple the law of sacrifice, and interpret it with a wide latitude in our own favour. What was said in the preceding chapter about the respective values of human and brute activities will go to justify as much of this as is justifiable; but it is certainly carried too far, and there is a great want of a fixed standard.

So far, the general principle of dealing with animals which is in a vague way accepted by most humane persons, but seldom distinctly formulated, seems to be that we may kill, inconvenience, or pain them, for any benefit, convenience, or pleasure to ourselves; but that the pain must be within moderate limits (of course undefined), and that it must form no element in our pleasure. For this I propose to substitute the far stricter rule, that we must commit no cruelty towards them,—defining cruelty as the infliction of pain without an adequate good object. This goes far beyond what is usually put in practice, and any one who tries to apply it in every case will find it a sufficiently stringent limitation. But it certainly does not come up to the new principle which we are asked† to recognize, even the same

* Sardines, white-bait, shrimps—compare the amount of food and the loss of life implied in the words. Fur trimmings, ornamental feathers, gloves—what is the proportion there between the satisfying of human needs and the destruction of animal enjoyment?

† By Mr. Hutton, *Nineteenth Century*, January, 1882, p. 37.

that we find it so hard to carry out towards our fellow-men, the golden rule of doing as we would be done by. We are told to "put ourselves in the place of the lower animals, and ask what we, with their pains, and their sensitiveness, and their prospects of life, and pain, and happiness, might fairly expect of beings of much greater power, but of common susceptibilities." This brings us to our fourth point, the infringement of the rights of animals; and we can best discuss it in discussing Mr. Hutton's proposed standard.

To begin with, such an effort of the imagination is almost impossible. If we transplant ourselves into the place of the lower animals, it is always *we* who are there; we, with our own susceptibilities, not theirs, and our intellects working up the raw material of their feelings. This is precisely what we see happening in a great deal that is written upon this subject. People talk about the rights of animals, and import into the discussion the very feeling of personal outrage and wrong which they themselves would have if any of their own were invaded. But the sense of individual rights is not even necessarily human. How much of it can a Fijian have, who stands still to be knocked on the head, because "the king has willed it;"[*] or a Dahomean, who belongs to a nation of which every man is the king's slave? Probably the Fijian does not *like* to be knocked on the head, any more than an ox does, but it is absurd to assume in the beast a sense of injury which is absent in the man. The fact is, that we can realize an animal's sensibility, but not its insensibility; its knowledge, but not its ignorance; its powers, but not their limitations. Nothing is more hopeless than the attempt to expel from our minds that with which we are perfectly familiar; the old knowledge will sneak in again at the back door of our argument, and we shall find

[*] Spencer's "Principles of Sociology," vol. i. p. 583.

it quietly underlying the most novel deduction. This is so with the sentence quoted from Mr. Hutton, where the innocent-looking words "fairly expect" involve the whole sense of mutual duty and personal right which is exclusively human, and which some races even of men have yet to be educated up to. We shall see this more clearly if we attempt to make the supposition which he proposes.

We must try, then, to imagine ourselves belonging to superior beings, who make us obey them in all things, and whose reasons we can seldom understand. They tie or shut us up, in order to prevent our going where we wish—they whip us, to make us go where they wish—they prevent our making love, for fear of its interfering with our work—they keep us in prisons, because they like to look at us and hear us sing—they take away our clothes, in order to wear them themselves—they crop our ears, because they think we look prettier with them short—they do various painful things to us, in order to make us taste nicer when cooked—and, finally, they kill and eat us. We are ignorant of most of their reasons for these unpleasant proceedings; but just in proportion as our intellects are developed and our characters fine, we acquiesce in this state of things, and are loving and loyal to our masters, with an unquestioning obedience and an unrebelling submission. But having come to this point, if we were suddenly enabled to understand the reasons for each action, our dispositions remaining the same, is it likely that the sense of injury which had not been evoked by anything else would arise when they went on to use us for experiments for the advancement of their science, and the improvement of their own health? If we were willing to be killed in order to support life as food, why should we object to die in order to preserve it by knowledge? Of course, it is an absurd supposition altogether; the confusion between what animals cannot possibly understand,

and what we should have to suppose ourselves in their place understanding, in order to pass judgment on the morality of their treatment—is inextricable, and altogether it is an idea that cannot be worked out; but the attempt to apply the "put yourself in his place" argument altogether fails to convince us that under any circumstances we should object most to the pain inflicted for the best reasons.

Mr. Hutton is willing to admit the inoculation class of experiments, "especially as these inoculations may well benefit not only man but the very creatures who suffer them." It is not clear whether he means the *individuals* which suffer, or the *kind of creatures*. If the former, the consideration has little force; because in every series of such experiments, the failures must be the majority,—for when marked success has been reached, the experiment is at an end. If the latter, it follows that he thinks it more moral to cause an animal pain for the sake of others of the same species than of others of a higher order. It is difficult to follow this reasoning, or to see what difference it would make to the creature concerned.

Let us gather up the scattered threads of this chapter.

We have proved that all creatures—human and other—live under the Law of Sacrifice; and that animals owe their physical prosperity—and men their social union and spiritual elevation—to this Law, in the first place submitted to unconsciously, in the latter accepted more or less deliberately.

We have seen that when we withdraw animals from the natural action of this Law, we apply it to them ourselves for our own interest, and that this is the condition of their being of value, use, or pleasure to us.

We have laid down for our guidance in dealing with them the rule of causing them no pain without an adequate good object, and have found it to be more stringent than any at present prevailing.

We have found it impossible to go further, and apply to them the Golden Rule, the differences in nature, sensibility, and intellect, being insuperable by the imagination.

But we have seen no reason to suppose that it can be lawful to give pain for purposes of human convenience, pleasure, business, or food,—and unlawful to give it for purposes of human health and knowledge.

We therefore conclude that *to make painful experiments upon living animals lies within an universally recognized right over them, and is not wrong in itself, but depends for its morality or immorality upon the circumstances and motives of each particular act.*

CHAPTER V.

WHAT IS VIVISECTION?

What is Vivisection?—Various definitions—Dissecting alive—True sense of the word—Course of study in physiological laboratories—Histological department—Chemical department—Physical department—Experiments upon detached tissue and organs—Experiments upon pithed animals—Painful experiments—Inoculations—Testing of drugs—Use of anæsthetics—Statistics of experiments performed—Conclusion.

WE have now made some progress in our inquiry. Having obtained a clear conception of what pain is, we have seen when its infliction is justifiable, and when it amounts to cruelty, and we have also decided that we have a right to inflict it upon the lower animals, when necessary for the purposes of beneficent science. We have to deal with an entire denial of that right, and a determined effort to abolish the power of using it. It therefore seems as if our next step should be to ask what use is made of it already. What is the state of affairs which it is proposed to improve upon? To what extent is vivisection practised in England?

But another question must come before this. What *is* vivisection? Literally, of course, the cutting of a living thing, such as opening an oyster, crimping a cod, or foxing a terrier. Sir Thomas Watson rather vaguely explains it as "the cutting into any living animal for scientific purposes."* "Vernon Lee"† says that "vivisection is a generic name for torture," an expression of which much meditation has hitherto failed to reveal the meaning. Webster's dictionary gives it as: "The dissection of an animal while alive, for the purpose of making physiological investigation." Probably this is a fair statement of the popular notion.‡ Many people suppose that—just as an anatomist lays bare nerve after nerve and muscle after muscle in a dead body, tracing each from its source to its remotest ramification, until he is thoroughly acquainted with its position and relations—so the physiologist studies the functions of living organs, displaying them and watching their working in the living body, and making each subject serve for as many experiments as possible, until death renders it useless. Nothing less than such an idea will justify the language used by some of the anti-vivisectionists about "the most cruel of cruelties." Still, it is rather out of date, for it is about two hundred years since it represented any existing fact. No doubt, the anatomists of the middle ages did cut open living bodies to see what was going on inside;§ but now, the coarser structure and general relationships of the principal organs are understood and taught on the dead human subject, which in olden times was out of the reach of the most skilled anatomist. As we shall see, there are other means of teaching the functions of the different parts of the body to students than the old actual vivisections. The experiments now performed on living animals are delicate and difficult; they require much time and expensive instruments; some of the most important involve very little operating; and there is nothing at all corresponding to

---

* Report of Royal Commission, Appendix III., § 1.
† *Contemporary Review*, May, 1882, p. 797.
‡ See Appendix A., ¶ 5.
§ The practice was recommended by Bacon, see Appendix C., ¶ 11.

dissection, or "cutting up." Webster's definition is therefore misleading, and the literal meaning is valueless for this discussion. One might speak of vivisecting a plant, for there is vegetable life as well as animal; and it is certainly vivisection to cut up tissue which is itself living, though removed from a dead animal. But this sort of thing is not what people mean when they talk about vivisection. They mean making any experiment upon animals which gives them pain, whether there is any *cutting* in it or not; they generally have some loose ideas about dissecting alive, like Mr. Webster's; and the more careless or dishonest of them throw in "torture" as a natural accompaniment, without waiting to inquire into the degree of pain caused. The word has thus become so vague as to be almost useless for purposes of argument, and I have hitherto tried to dispense with it as far as possible, and shall continue to do so; but if I am obliged to use it, it will always be in the true sense of *cutting a living thing*, whether animal or vegetable, sentient or insentient, an organism or a part of an organism. When experiments on living animals are in question, it is easy to call them by their right name.

Only a small part of the work done in physiological laboratories consists of such experiments, but though their proportion to the rest is small in quantity, it is large in importance. Both statements will be best explained by a short review of the various sections into which Practical Physiology is divided, both in text-books and in teaching establishments. These will usually be found to be four: *i.e.*, the Histological, Chemical, Physical, and Vital departments.[*]

In the Histological department, the pupil studies—by means of the microscope—the minute structure of the tissues of animals and plants. The living animals examined

---

[*] See "The Practice of Vivisection in England," by Professor Yeo. —*Fortnightly Review*, March 1, 1882.

are (with very few exceptions) tiny animalculæ, which swim about under the glass with every appearance of ease, and do not seem to consider themselves victims to science. The common exception is the frog, the web of whose foot is spread out under the object-glass, that the course of the living blood-corpuscles through its transparent substance may be observed. In this case there is no -*section* at all, and the animal is not injured in any way. It is wrapped in damp cloths, and its toes are held apart by soft threads attached to their tips. Every precaution must be taken against hurting the frog, or irritating its toes with the thread, or even the moderate heat of the human hand,—as the least roughness or want of skill in operating would interfere with the value of the observation, by increasing or checking the flow of the blood in the delicate vessels. A small portion of living tissue is often studied in this department, but then it has been taken from dead animals. Every one, perhaps, may not know that the tissues have an independent life, which may survive for some time the death of the organism, if that has taken place while they were in health. In this way, the movements of the living cells of man's blood, the contracting of insects' muscles, and many other vital phenomena, may be observed. This study of life without a living creature is not vivisection in the popular sense; on the contrary, it is necessary that the animal from which the tissues are taken should have been killed as rapidly as possible. On the whole, then, it is clear that in the histological department, which constitutes, probably, a fourth of the whole laboratory work, and is the first and most important division of that work in which students have to take an active part—there are no painful experiments, and the vivisections performed are only upon little bits of tissue, and not upon animals.

We next come to the Chemical department. Here the

student learns the nature and composition of the secretions and excretions, how to test them, and judge of their character,—knowledge that will be most important to him in diagnosing disease, but in gaining which he works on fluids brought to him in the laboratory, collected painlessly from living human beings, or extracted from the gland-textures of dead animals. Here there is no cause of dispute.

What I have called the Physical department is that in which the forces of nature are studied in their relation to vital phenomena. The student is provided with an elementary knowledge of the laws of dynamics and mechanics, sufficient to make him understand the action of the atmosphere in its pressure upon the lungs, the working of the muscles as levers, the principle of the pumping of blood through the body by the heart, &c. Here also mechanical appliances are introduced, to explain the working of the organs, and to investigate and accurately measure the actions of various parts of the body. Models are shown, illustrating the process of breathing, the alternate contraction and expansion of the heart, the wonderful movements of the eyeball,—and the apparatus by which a ray of light is refracted, so as exactly to meet the ending of the optic nerve, and excite visual sensations. The very *raison d'être* of all these expensive and elaborate models and instruments—is to dispense with vivisection. Artificial lungs and mechanical eyeballs would be merely curiosities of inventions, if professors were in the habit of exposing the actual palpitating organs to their pupils' gaze, in the body of a living animal.

The instruments for measuring the action of certain organs are indeed used upon living animals, but there is no pain in their application, and the subjects are generally human. The *cardiograph* writes down the manner in which the heart beats, the *sphygmograph* registers the character of the pulse, and the *ophthalmoscope* enables the surgeon to explore the recesses of the eye, and judge of the condition of the nerve itself. The student learns the use of these instruments as well as of the laryngoscope and the thermometer for his future bed-side practice; but the inconvenience which he inflicts in the process is very trifling, whether he experiments on himself, his relatives at home, his fellow-students, or the lower animals. At any rate, nothing takes place in the Physical department which need excite any horror, or raise any moral discussion.

The fourth department is that in which the painful experiments on living animals take place, but they are very far from forming the whole of its work. As in histological investigation, experiments are often made upon living tissue from a dead creature, so here the laws which govern the action of the heart, nerves, and muscles, can be to a great extent studied in organs removed from a recently killed animal. If a frog be beheaded,* and its heart extracted, the heart will continue to beat for hours after it has been separated from the body, and influences which will quicken or retard its action may be tried upon it. Nerve-fibre can be stimulated, and muscle will contract after they have been taken from an animal thus killed, and their actions can be excellently studied.† Much that was first discovered by vivisection can now be shown and explained in this painless but effective manner; and in our English schools it *is* so explained, and a living creature is never used where a dead one will do.

Next in order to these experiments upon organs, come experiments upon entire animals, deprived of consciousness and partially of life, by pithing. The creature is put under

* This mode of death leaves the reflex phenomena of the spinal cord in fullest operation.

† See Memorandum issued by the Association for the Advancement of Medicine by Research, p. 6.

an anæsthetic, and the spinal marrow is divided. The nervous centres which preside over the breathing movements are thus injured, so that it would die, if oxygen were not supplied to its blood : but by means of a kind of air-pump, artificial respiration is kept up, the heart continues to beat, and functional life is maintained. Still, as has been fully shown in Chap. II., the animal is not really alive; for it is not capable of spontaneous action, and all sensation has been destroyed, by cutting the communication between the brain and the nerves of the body. The whole apparatus is in the condition of a telegraphic circuit with the wires and battery perfect, but with no operator to work them : there is still receptivity in the instrument, energy in the battery, and conductility in the wire, but there is no spontaneity of action, and there can be no message.

We now come to experiments more nearly corresponding to the popular idea of vivisection; *i.e.*, those which involve incision or cutting, are performed on living creatures, and are of a nature to give pain, if the subject is not prevented from feeling it. To begin with, it cannot be too often repeated, that *in England animals are never "cut up" at all, nor are they dissected alive in order to show the relations of their parts.* This is taught, as has been already explained, by means of dead subjects, models, and diagrams. When vivisections are performed for teaching purposes, they are done in order to show to students something necessary for them to know, but which they cannot be taught equally well otherwise; and under the present law anæsthetics must always be used at such demonstrations. So that there is no room for talking about medical students being demoralized by witnessing tortures : there are none for them to witness. Vivisections in original researches are performed only when the question in hand cannot be solved by chemistry, histology, or any other of the means at command, and always with a definite object in view. The "random experiment" under which we hear of creatures expiring in torment, exists only in the minds of certain excitable but ill-informed writers.

Painful vivisections are therefore confined to purposes of original research, and in the few cases where pain must be given, it is generally very slight. One large class consists of inoculations, which are chiefly used in studying the origin and communication of diseases. There are a few pricks and scratches, giving about as much pain as vaccination: and if the disease expected is induced, the subject is usually killed at once, unless kept alive to try modes of treatment. In the former case, it does not suffer; in the latter, it is carefully nursed and doctored; and as most sick people prefer being treated to being extinguished, we may fairly suppose that an inoculated rabbit would gladly countersign a certificate to permit the doctor to keep it alive.

Another large class of experiments consists in trying the effects of drugs upon animals, as a guide to their use upon human patients; or, in the case of poisons, to study their antidotes and treatment. They are generally administered by injection under the skin, and the —section consists only in pinching up a portion of it, and inserting the pointed nozzle of a syringe. The pain of the actual operation is merely a prick, but that which results will be more or less, according to the nature and action of the drug.

There then remain a number of experiments which cannot be further classified, relating to the various animal functions, varying according to the points which scientific men desire to ascertain, and which the Home Secretary does not consider useless knowledge. In most of these, anæsthetics can be used. Whenever they can be used they are, and always were, before any law was passed on the subject. This was proved abundantly before the Royal Commission, and is recognized in their report. Yet, although no fact is better authenticated than this systematic narcotizing of creatures experimented on,* it is quietly and constantly ignored, vivisection is described as the "worst form of cruelty we know,"† and the words "agony," "torture," and "torment" are scattered about as if no such things existed as chloroform, ether, and morphia. But this is contrary to common sense. If an experimenter did not use them for the sake of humanity, he would for his own convenience. Can any one suppose that it is agreeable to a man conducting a difficult investigation to have the subject crying and restless, when he requires perfect stillness for the sake of his delicate instruments, and undisturbed concentration for his own mind? An anæsthetic of some sort is absolutely necessary for the success of most operations, and equally needful for the feelings of most operators. Doctors are men,—men, the whole object of whose lives is to relieve suffering, who live to heal and soothe, and whose feelings are constantly cultivated by demands on their help and sympathy, their skill and tenderness. Working physiologists share these influences. They are not a caste of Fakeers, cut off from all the gentlenesses of life, and vowed neither to pity themselves nor others. They have at home not only their wives and families, but the little child's pet kitten, the devoted dog, their own favourite horse,—all the friendly animal world which gathers round an English home, seldom so poor that it does not hold a pet. Why should it be supposed that they *like* to hurt a helpless creature lying at their mercy? As a matter of fact, they do not; and Mr. Colam's often-quoted evidence ‡ is alone sufficient to show

---

* See Digest of Replies to Questions forwarded to the principal Medical Schools.—Report of Royal Commission, Appendix III., § 8.

† Miss Cobbe, in *Contemporary Review*, February, 1877.

‡ See Appendix B, ¶ 4.

that no such charge against them could for one instant be supported. If anæsthetics are not constantly mentioned in text-books, it is because their use in every laboratory is taken for granted.*

But experiments are sometimes performed without anæsthetics? That is true; it can be done under a special certificate; and let us now see to what extent—under the law as it stands—it *is* done. We have the reports presented to Parliament of the experiments performed in the years 1878, 1879, and 1880. In the report for 1878, the inspector says: "In 16 cases alone, so far as I am able to judge (and these were confined to two sets of experiments), is there any reason to believe that any considerable amount of suffering was directly inflicted." In 24 cases, animals suffered, not from an actual operation, but from induced disease. The report for 1879 states: "The number of experiments in which there is reason to believe that any material suffering was caused appears to have been about 25. Of these, 15 were cases in which disease followed the inoculation of infectious matter, but in which no painful operation was performed; and 10 were experiments upon as many frogs, in which an incision of the skin was required for the introduction beneath it of a medical substance." The account for 1880 is similar. In about 30 instances disease was induced, "which, during the brief period the animals survived, may have caused slight suffering." There were no other painful experiments.†

This then is the sum total of the pain-giving experiments upon animals performed in England during three years. Less than 100 cases, of which the great majority consist of inoculations, followed—not by torture, but—by illness, form the contribution of our country to the "systematic torturing of thousands of beasts all over the world,"

* See Appendix B, ¶ 4. † See Appendix B, ¶ 5

referred to by a writer on the subject.* It is a pity that 95 animals should have been put to any discomfort at all; and if illness and pain could be abolished from the world at one blow, the happiness of the lower creatures would be no small ingredient in the general joy. As it is, however, physiologists must aim at something humbler; they must try to decrease what they cannot destroy, and to alleviate where they cannot heal. And those who wish to narrow the means at their command for doing so, by totally prohibiting experiments on living animals,† had better be quite sure that they know what the state of things is which they propose to alter. The same writer says that "experimentations on living animals is a system of long protracted agonies, the very recollection of which is enough to make the soul sick as with a whiff and an aftertaste from a moral sewer." The degree of correspondence between this phrase and the facts of English physiological practice will be apparent to the reader of the foregoing pages. And it is with facts alone that we wish to deal.

* *Contemporary Review*, May, 1882, p. 803.
† A Bill for the total Abolition of Vivisection is to be presented to Parliament this Session.

CHAPTER VI.

THE RELATION OF EXPERIMENT TO PHYSIOLOGY.*

Many non-physiological systems—Only one physiological system—The Empirical system—The physiological system founded on experiment —Experiment on living animals part of a rational method of investigation—The Circulation of the Blood—Blood pressure—Contractile power of the arteries—The Absorbent Vessels—Discoveries of Aselli and Pecquet—Value of this knowledge—Respiration—Changes effected in the inspired air—Changes effected in the blood—Digestion—The Nervous System—Discoveries of Bell, Magendie, and others—Present state of our knowledge on the subject—Muscular action—Discoveries of Heller—Summary.

SINCE human beings first writhed under the ills that flesh is heir to, and strove to escape from them, various different systems of medicine have won the confidence and relieved or aggravated the sufferings of mankind. However many they are, they must all fall into one of two classes—the physiological and the non-physiological. Physiological medicine is founded upon study of the organs of the body and their modes of action : that is, upon a knowledge—the more thorough the better—of the mechanism with which it has to deal. Although, as long as this knowledge is imperfect, different conclusions may be drawn from

* For the information contained in this and the following chapter, I am largely indebted to an Address delivered before the Surgical Society of Ireland in 1878, by Dr. Robert McDonnell, to Professor Heidenhain's Pamphlet, " *Die Vivisection im Dienst der Heilkunde,*" Leipzig, 1879, and to the Arris and Gale Lectures of 1882, delivered by Professor Gerald F. Yeo, and published in the *Lancet,* June 10, 1882, *et seq.*

it, and different methods of treatment proposed and tried, so that it may seem as if there were various physiological systems, yet in reality there is but one; for all physiological workers acknowledge the same principles, and can correct and supplement each other's work,—so that the mistakes of yesterday are set right by the discoveries of to-day, and these will be developed by the results of to-morrow. It is not so with the non-physiological systems. These are many and various, and are based upon principles which are mutually irreconcileable. Nearly all of them, also, have their modern representatives, but I shall not risk bringing all these down upon me at once by specifying their parentage.

In the earliest times, when every disease was attributed to the anger or malice of some spirit, the only system of medicine known consisted in attempts to propitiate the offended power. Later on, under the influence of Greek intellect, this gave rise to something more deserving of the name. The origin of the empirical system of medicine is very interesting, and it certainly has a solid foundation, since it rests upon the observation of facts. The priests of some of the Greek temples (certainly of that at Cos) to which people used to resort in search of miraculous cures, kept records of the names of the patients, their diseases, and the means (other than miraculous) taken to cure them. These were inscribed upon metal plates, called votive tablets, and were carefully preserved. Hippocrates, himself a priest of Cos, formed the accumulated experience of the temple into his great system, which at least, as has been said, rested on facts and nature. The empirical school has had varied fortunes, sometimes sinking into mere vulgar blundering, and sometimes having the success which attended the patient listening to nature, in days when men did not know how to question her. But the mere collection of information without reasoning upon it is simply useless, and a hundred disjointed facts will no more make one truth than a bag-full of acorns will make one oak. One of those seeds, planted in the right soil, and duly tended, may grow into a noble tree; and one of those facts, in the mind of a man of genius, capable of seeing its relations and working out its results, may lead to a great discovery. Thus empiricism—or the mere observation of nature—never created, or could create, a sound system of physiology. It is a system of hits and misses, free from humbug, but not trustworthy; because it works on the supposition that one case will be exactly like another, whereas no one case ever *is* exactly like another.

It would take a volume to sketch the various non-physiological systems, and the results to unfortunate patients, in days when there was no such thing as systematic physiology. For there is no third alternative. So far as the physician knows the structure of the body with which he has to deal, the relations of its functions and the working of its organs in health,—so far as he can recognize disease, trace its causes and consequences, and calculate upon the effect of the treatment which he adopts —so far he is working in the light, and is likely to succeed. But so far as he is guessing, theorizing, and experimenting on his patient,—so far he is groping in the dark, and is likely to fail. These seem very elementary truths, but it is sometimes necessary to insist on the most obvious things, when they are overlooked; and the defenders of science are obliged to spend such eloquence, research, and time, as are at their command—in defending this apparently unassailable position: It is necessary that a doctor should know what he is doing. Or, in scientific language: Rational therapeutics are based upon sound physiology.

But *is* the physiological system of medicine firmly

founded upon knowledge that can be relied upon? and if so, what share has experiment had in attaining this knowledge?

To begin with, it must be noted that experiment upon living animals is not a thing by itself. It is part of a system—the physiological system, and part of a method—the experimental method. No great discoverer was ever a vivisector, and nothing more, though every great physiological discoverer has been a vivisector. He did not spend his time in the "random experiment" in which his profession are supposed to delight; he had something better to do with it. While his mind was open to all ideas, his thoughts were bent on one; he learnt what anatomy could teach him of the matter in question; he watched by sick beds, and observed accidental circumstances; he studied the doings of other workers, and meditated upon them; he probably—if the subject admitted of it—experimented on himself. All these things—anatomy, clinical observation, and meditation—are absolutely necessary; but they are parts of an accurate and scientific manner of investigation which cannot dispense with the additional means of experiment on living animals. For it is really the touchstone by which the theories starting from the other methods are judged, and the results obtained from them are studied.

In order to trace, as briefly as possible, consistently with clearness, the dependence of physiology upon experiment, let us take in turn some of the great branches of such knowledge, and inquire what were the earliest ideas held on these subjects, what knowledge upon them we have arrived at, and what share experiment has had in leading us to this point. For the sake of brevity, it will be understood that experiment means experiment upon living animals, unless otherwise stated. Of course, I must assume in my readers such a general knowledge of elementary physiology as every educated person ought to possess; without which it would be absurd for any one to attempt to form an opinion on the subject of vivisection.

To begin, then, with the Circulation of the Blood. It is difficult to take ourselves in imagination back to a time when the use of the arteries was utterly unknown. Yet Erasistratus, who preceded Galen, thought that they contained nothing but air. Galen (who flourished about 131-201 A.D.) was a diligent experimenter, and vivisection soon taught him that this was not the fact. He says: "If one cut many arteries at the same time, they will all let blood escape. This is a fact known to all the world." He, however, thought that they carried both blood and air; and that their chief business was to conduct air (or *vital spirits*, as he called it,) from the heart to vivify the whole body. The nourishing material from the food was collected (according to his views) by the gastric and intestinal veins, and carried to the liver, where it was made into blood, which was then distributed to the various parts of the body by the systemic veins. Some of the fresh blood coming from the liver flowed through the right side of the heart, and was conveyed to nourish the lungs, by the pulmonary artery. He thought that the current flowed backwards and forwards in the arteries and veins alike, the former carrying the nutritive, the latter the vital blood.

This curious mixture of fact and fancy was all that was attained by the first great experimental physiologist,* and it is noticeable that the facts are clearly due to vivisection, which alone could have shown him the presence of the blood-flow in the vessels, and which convinced him (in spite

* We know that experiment formed a part of Egyptian medicine, but with our present imperfect knowledge of the state of that science in Ancient Egypt, this must be passed over.

of his former theory) that all the arteries contained blood. Although he had gone thus far in 200 A.D., yet at the beginning of the 17th century, we find knowledge of this subject in much the same position. The great motor power of the heart was unknown, the direction and constancy of the flow of blood through the vessels of the system had not been ascertained, and the circulation through the liver was a complete mystery. How was this? Had not doctors been practising, binding up wounds, observing patients, and reflecting upon what they saw, during those fourteen centuries? They had; but they had not been experimenting. *Vivisectors* there were, in the true sense of the word, who really dissected animals alive, in order to study the parts of the body; but these were anatomists, not physiologists. The few experiments that were performed were not sufficiently numerous, careful, or systematic, to produce any result worth mentioning. In 1628, Harvey picked up the wonder-working rod that had fallen from the hand of Galen, and physiology moved on again.

It was more than a move; it was the greatest stride that the science ever took at one time. The discovery of the Circulation of the Blood was to Physiology what that of the Law of Gravitation was to Physics.

Let us learn from his own words how he arrived at it.*

"When, *in many dissections of living things* (as were given to hand) I first applied my mind to observation, whereby I might discover the wont and utilities of the heart's motion by personal inspection, and not by the books and writings of others, I found it a hard subject indeed, and so

---

* As the verbal accuracy of Dr. Willis's excellent translation has been impugned, I give a baldly literal version, in order to minimize causes of dispute. The question of Harvey's priority is discussed in Appendix D, ¶ 1.

constantly full of difficulties that with Fracastorius, I might almost think the motion of the heart to be known to God alone. For neither in what way systole or diastole might take place nor when, or where dilatation and contraction might exist, could I rightly distinguish, on account of the rapidity of the motion, which in many animals in the twinkling of an eye—as if in a flash of lightning—brought itself into view and straightway vanished; so that I might think now I perceived systole on this side, diastole on that, at another time the contrary, the motions to become various and confused; whereby my mind fluctuated, and I could not come to any resolution myself, or believe others, and I was not astonished that Andrew Laurentius wrote that the motion of the heart was what the flow and ebb of the Euripus was to Aristotle. At length, from day to day using greater research, and diligence, *by frequently looking into many and various living animals*, I thought to have both attained the object, and to have escaped from this labyrinth, and at the same time to have discovered things which I desired, the motion and wont of the heart and arteries. From which I was not afraid to put forward my opinion in this matter not only to my friends in public, but also in my anatomical lectures, in the Academic method."*

Harvey did not know all the details of the course pursued by the blood, especially of the manner in which it made its way from the arteries into the veins. Malpighi, who was the father of minute anatomy, was the first to see it in the capillary vessels, and he demonstrated its passage through the capillary network of the lung of a living frog by a genuine vivisection, thus adding the last link to Harvey's chain of evidence.

Comparatively recently, the experiments of Waller and

* "*De Motu Cardis et Sanguinis.*" Cap. I.

Cohnheim have taught us that the walls of the capillaries will allow the solid—as well as the fluid—parts of the blood to pass through them; and as a white corpuscle has been seen to creep through the thin walls of the vessel, we now know that not only does the blood convey nourishment to the tissues, but that these mysterious little units of protoplasm, which are the active agents in the formation of new tissue, can start from it on their work of re-creation.

The pressure of the blood against the walls of the arteries was first studied by Dr. Stephen Hales, vicar of Teddington. In 1732 he published his Statical Essays, in which he described the experiments by which he estimated the force of the heart. His methods of measurement were improved upon by Poiseuille, and the whole subject of hæmo-dynamics (or the force of the blood) was fundamentally investigated by Volkmann. Of course, it could only be studied upon living animals. As a result of these investigations and experiments, there are now a number of instruments (the kymograph, sphygmograph, and cardiograph,) which enable physicians to observe—and record graphically—the most delicate changes in the circulation, and are most valuable in studying the fluctuations of disease.

Just when the discovery of the immense pumping-power of the heart was threatening to degrade the arteries into mere conduit-pipes, it was discovered by Haller that they possessed a distinct coat of muscle-tissue and an independent power of contracting, so as to press upon the blood which they contained. John Hunter's experiments upon the horse, and Dr. John Thomson's demonstrations on the frog's web, put the matter beyond doubt. Claude Bernard, Brown-Séquard, and other experimenters, gradually showed the wonderful muscular and nervous systems by which this contractility is produced and governed, and which are constantly at work, regulating the blood-supply to the various organs.

Let us now sum up what amount of our knowledge of the blood and its circulation is due to experiments upon living animals. In this manner we have learnt that the arteries contain blood (Galen)—that it is driven into them by the pumping action of the heart under high pressure, and so forced through the body, and that the veins collect it and return it to the heart (Harvey)—that it passes from the arteries to the veins through the capillaries (Malpighi and Leeuwenhoeck)—and that it conveys solid nourishment and formative agents to the tissues (Waller and Cohnheim). We can measure exactly the force of its pressure against the vessels which contain it (Hales, Poiseuille, Volkmann); and we understand the manner in which these vessels contract and dilate, and the nervous system which causes them to do so. It would be quite impossible, in a little book like this, to show in detail the influence which these experiments have had upon medical practice, and how clear an insight they have given physicians into the true interpretation of the various kinds of pulse, the changes in the heart's beat, &c. The question to be asked is not—When is such knowledge as this useful? but—What act or conclusion in medical practice is independent of it? And another question is—How will those earnest anti-vivisectionists, who, like Miss Cobbe, prefer to "die sooner than profit by such foul rites," provide themselves with a medical attendant warranted ignorant of the circulation of the blood?

Very closely connected with the circulation of the blood are the flow of the chyle and lymph in their special capillaries and peculiarly delicate vessels, and the nature of the absorbent system generally. The subject was not at all understood in the time of Harvey, and a hot controversy was raging as to whether or not the absorption of chyle was the sole business of the mesenteric blood-vessels, when a great Italian anatomist, Gaspardus Asellius, suddenly chanced upon the solution of the whole question. On the 23rd of July, 1662, he was making an experiment upon a dog which had lately had a full meal,* when he observed " a number of very fine white cords," which he at first supposed to be nerves, but which, when pierced, proved to contain a milky fluid. The discovery which he had made then burst upon him, and he saw that he had hit upon the conduits by which the chyle was conveyed to the blood But he was not successful in tracing their subsequent course correctly; and, as he held to the old idea that all nutrient matter was carried to the liver, there to be made into blood, he was easily satisfied that the lacteals which he had discovered led to that organ.

By a chance precisely similar to that which had revealed the lacteals to Asellius,† Jean Pecquet happened—while experimenting for another purpose—to observe the opening of the main absorbent vessel of the thoracic duct, which carries their contents into the blood current. He followed up the clue thus given him, and by repeated experiments succeeded in tracing the general course of the lymphatic system.‡ The numerous experiments of Hunter, Hewson, Cruikshank, and Magendie, have given us a clear idea of the mechanism by which food is absorbed from the alimentary canal and poured into the blood, and of the wide distribution of these absorbent vessels, and their other functions in collecting and carrying away the overflow of nutrient fluid from the textures. It is through experiment—and experiment alone

---

* For detailed account in Asellius's own words, see Appendix D. ¶ 2.
† For detailed account in Pecquet's own words, see Appendix D. ¶ 2.
‡ For a different account of the matter, see Appendix D. ¶ 2.

—that we know the course and uses of the lacteals and other absorbent vessels, know that they bring to the blood nourishment from the alimentary tract, as well as some waste products and superfluous fluid from the tissues; and know, too, that by their means foreign matter can be passed into the system. The method of hypodermic injection of drugs rests upon the knowledge of their presence and efficiency; and what a wonderful amount of relief and healing must be counted to that invention alone! And if the only result of these experiments had been to make it possible for surgeons to use a catgut ligature that can be absorbed, instead of one of silk or other material, which (as a rule) must be removed with pain and risk, after many months of irritating delay, they would have conferred a very great boon upon surgery, and even a greater upon surgical patients.

The processes of Respiration were not so soon traced out as those of the two circulations. The ancients believed that the air passed through the lung into the cavity of the chest, thence to pass on into the heart, where it mingled with the blood. This opinion was held in the beginning of the 17th century, and by such men as Harvey, Hales, and Boerhaave. The mistake survived, because their knowledge was taken partly from experimentation upon birds and partly from the examination of bodies after death—with which practical physiology is now enjoined to content herself. But a lung dead and collapsed is as like a lung living and inflated as an empty balloon is like a full one, and the conclusions drawn from the one for the other were proportionately trustworthy. Haller, however, carried out a series of experiments which disproved this fallacy. Malpighi's experiments showed the vesicular texture of the lungs, and the manner in which the blood was exposed in a network of minute vessels to the air which they contained, and made the air-cells familiar to physiologists. The nature of the change which took place in the capillaries of the lungs still, however, remained a mystery.

Mayow, by acute reasoning, and a most carefully arranged series of experiments (for the most part upon living animals), arrived at conclusions far in advance of his time, when but few of the chemical elements were known. He pronounced atmospheric air to be a compound, containing as one of its elements a body to which he attributed the properties possessed by oxygen, but which he called (on account of its relation to nitric acid) *nitro-œrial spirit*. This alone it was which made the air useful for combustion and respiration. The times, however, were not ripe for the reception of his discoveries, and they were neglected.

Later on, in the year 1759, Black showed by experiments the presence of what is now known as carbonic acid in the expired air; and in 1770 Priestley proved in the same manner the analogy of respiration to combustion, and concluded that air in its passage through the lungs lost some of its oxygen. But Lavoisier was the first to give an exact explanation of the chemical changes which occur in the process of breathing; and this he was enabled to do by his skilful and diligent experimentation. The more important of his principles have been worked out and confirmed by others, also experimentally; so that we now know even the exact quantities of carbonic acid given off and oxygen used up in respiration.

So much for the changes in the inspired air worked by its contact with the blood; but what change in the blood is effected by the air? This question also was answered by experiment. The difference of colour between the blood in the veins and that in the arteries had been noticed from the earliest times; but the first real light thrown upon the subject emanated from an admirable series of experiments made by Lower, who opened the thorax of a living animal, and discovered that the change in colour took place in the capillaries of the lungs. This discovery was not, however, followed up, and it was Priestley whose experiments actually convinced the world that the alteration was due to the purifying of the blood by means of the oxygen of the air.

Let us again sum up our debt to experiment. Imagine any doctor trying to treat a consumptive patient on the supposition that the lungs let the air through into the cavity which contains them! From such ignorance of facts, and all the consequent blundering in practice, experiment— and experiment alone—has delivered us. Haller thus demolished the pleural-cavity mistake; while Malpighi had shown the texture of the lungs, and the manner in which the blood and air were brought into contact, by observing under the microscope the lungs of a living frog; Mayow learnt the action of oxygen; Black demonstrated the presence of carbonic acid in expired air; Priestley proved the loss of oxygen in breathing, inferred the analogy of respiration to combustion, and confirmed and explained Lower's discovery that the change of colour in the blood took place in the capillaries of the lungs; Lavoisier gave a comprehensive explanation of the whole process; and later experimenters have ascertained the quantities of each gas subtracted from or added to the air in respiration. This is what experiment has taught us. If all this knowledge about respiration could be wiped out of our minds, and we were left only to what has been learnt by bedside observation, anatomy, and meditation, where would be our improved ventilation, and what efforts should we make to keep a proper amount of cubic space for a number of human beings living clustered together? Would not the pestilences known as gaol fever, war typhus, and hospital gangrene be still raging among our prisoners, our soldiers, and our poor, because we should know no reason why the same air should not be used again and again?

Various theories on the subject of digestion succeeded one another before experiment acquainted us with its true processes. It was at first attributed entirely to the moisture and heat of the stomach, which produced an action called "concoction." Next, it was referred to a process analogous to putrefaction, or believed to be the result only of trituration. The stomach had been supposed in turn to be a forcing-stove, a rotting-place, and a mill; and we might now have been thinking it a galvanic battery, if experiment had been unlawful some three hundred years ago. Spallanzani and Stephens, however, proved by this means the secretion of the gastric juice, and its effects upon different kinds of food. They were the first investigators in this direction, and it would be impossible to name all their successors,—so numerous and so rich in results have been their researches. It must be enough to say that all our present accurate knowledge of the gastric juice, its effect upon proteid food-stuffs, and its inertness for others, as well as the wide-spread activity of the pancreas (the function of which was so utterly unknown to the ancients), we owe to experiment of comparatively recent date.

The view of the nervous system held by the ancients was that the brain was a large gland, secreting certain animal spirits, which were distributed by the nerves to the different tissues of the body. "The nerves," says Galen, "like streams from a fountain, convey to the muscles their power from the brain." Experiment had given him a rough but fairly correct idea of the course of this stream of power, especially as conveyed by the spinal cord. He gave public demonstrations on the matter, using young pigs as subjects, that he might not shock the susceptibilities of the audience by employing the more human monkeys, which he would himself have preferred. He showed the effects on the respiratory system and other movements produced by section of the cord in the region of the neck; and he pointed out the results of section at other points, and in various manners. Considering how much he discovered concerning the spinal cord and its uses, it would seem incomprehensible that for seventeen centuries no important step in advance was taken towards understanding the true constitution of the nervous system; but then, they were seventeen centuries in which no accurate experiments were made upon this subject.

Galen's idea that the nerves were conduits of a fluid termed " vital spirits " held the field for a long time; but as this vital fluid was difficult of detection, it gradually ceased to be an object of belief, and the more correct idea gained ground—that the nerves transmitted vibrations. In their marvel at the first discovery of electricity, people were disposed to attribute everything to it, and it was then believed to be the source of these vibrations. Indeed, makers of electric bands and stockings still continue to advertise that " Electricity is Life." We are as far as ever from knowing what Life is; but, in consequence of experiments, we now know that nerve-impulse is a chemical change —not an electric current—taking place in the protoplasm of the nerve, and transmitted from one molecule to another along its delicate central strand.

As to the functions of the nerves, little progress was made from the days of Galen to those of Sir Charles Bell, Magendie, and Johannes Müller. The great idea of the motor functions of the efferent nerves, so brilliantly struck out by Sir Charles Bell in his few but valuable experiments, was worked out, confirmed, and developed by Magendie into a consistent theory of the two classes of nerves with their distinct functions; and it was chiefly by investigating the roots of the spinal nerves, in experiments upon frogs, that Johannes Müller arrived at his accurate conclusions as to the functions of the spinal cord. While the greatest credit is due to Marshall Hall for originality in discovering and persistence in teaching the laws of reflex action which really form the basis of our present knowledge of the uses of the nervous centres. We now know something of the actual constitution of the nerves; we know their relation to the brain, and the manner in which they bring impulses to and receive them from it; we are acquainted with their reflex action, and with the powerful influence of the spinal cord; and in the brain itself we know the situations of the cells and groups of cells which preside over many of our most important organic motions, such as breathing, swallowing, &c. At this point, investigation has been arrested in England by the fiat of the Secretary of State. But is it not obvious that without the knowledge already gained by this means, there could be no prospect at all of coping with the increasing nerve-maladies of our time? It is a knowledge still very incomplete, but which will continue to advance, if—but only if—experiment is not obliged to stand still.

Muscular action was attributed by Galen and his successors to the brain and spinal cord. "This is proved distinctly," he says, "by the fact that if you divide any of the nerves, or the spinal marrow itself, the part above the incision and in continuity with the brain will still retain its powers; but the part below will be incapable of producing either sense or motion." Glisson was the first to dissent from this view; he applied the term *irritability* to a muscle as distinct from its nerve, and seems to have had an idea of reflex action. Haller, however, (who, like Glisson, was an experimenter) explained the matter much more clearly. He taught us that every muscular fibre contracts when irritated, and that it is thus distinguished from vegetable fibre, which has no such power. This is the cause of muscular motions after death, for the irritability remains for a certain time, so that the muscles can be caused to contract. This irritability of the muscular fibre is independent of the nerves, and cannot be referred to any other power; its origin is quite unknown to us. Its effects, however, are not; and they form one of the principal data of surgery.

We have now gone in order through six of the principal branches of physiology, and we have found that in each the most important discoveries have been made by means of experiment, and that to it we owe the accuracy and certainty of whatever knowledge we possess. It is impossible to lay too much stress upon this point, for it is the stronghold of the case. Those who defend physiological experiment as an absolute necessity to medicine do so—not because this or that drug has been discovered by its means, this or that operation perfected through its practice. They defend it, because without it medicine is based upon ignorance, and every doctor is a charlatan, patching at a wonderful mechanism of which he knows nothing. They defend it, because it is the foundation upon which physiology as a science stands.* The pseudo-sciences rest upon theorizing, guess-work, and empiricism; a true science rests upon experiment. If physiology be deprived of this necessary foundation, it will be degraded through no fault of its disciples; it will not fall to pieces, because that which has been won cannot be taken away, but it will be unable to encroach any further upon the morass of human ignorance, because forbidden to lay a firm footing for its advancing tread. But, after all, interests differ. There are some who do not much care for that morass to be invaded. "Quand on veut dessécher un marais, on ne fait pas voter les grenouilles."†

---

* See Appendix C.   † Madame Emile de Girardin.

CHAPTER VII.

THE RELATION OF MEDICINE TO EXPERIMENT.

The subject a complicated one—An amputation in old times—An amputation at the present day—Facial nerves—Artificial respiration—Transfusion of blood—Orthopædic surgery—Internal operations—Chassaignac's *écraseur*—Removal of one kidney—Removal of larynx—"Animal grafting"—Study of the processes of disease—Testing of drugs—Preventive medicine—Other benefits of experiment.

THE facts given in the preceding chapter form by far the strongest proof of the value of experiment upon living animals; because they show the part that it has taken in building up—and therefore the part that it is likely to take in perfecting—the science of physiology, upon which all true medicine is based.*

* "Rational therapeutics must grow out of physiological knowledge, as surely as a plant is the outgrowth of its roots. As the remote rootlets are the exact parts which are all-important for the nutrition of the plant, so experiment feeds physiology, and thereby nourishes the art of medical practice. It would appear silly to ask to what rootlet any single fruit or flower on a widely-spreading tree owed its existence or nutrition ; and so it is idle to expect that each, or even any, therapeutic agent or method of diagnosis should be traced to the definite experimental discoveries that may have led to its adoption or use. As the branches of our medical tree spread wider and wider, and its diagnostic flowers and therapeutic fruits become more and more numerous, we find that its physiological roots go deeper and deeper in search of pabulum, and the experimental rootlets become still further removed from the more obviously useful and prolific part of the plant."—Arris and Gale Lectures, III., *Lancet*, August 5th, 1882, p. 175.

In such an inquiry, it was not very difficult to know when we had found what we were seeking for. Discoverers have usually given clear accounts of what they learnt, and how they learnt it; and a fact in physiology can be proved, tested, and verified, as thoroughly as one in chemistry. Either the lacteals do or do not empty themselves into the thoracic duct; either the efferent nerve will convey motor impulses, or it will not. There may be a mistake about such matters, but there can be no uncertainty. When the truth has once been found out, it is not likely to be questioned again; and so it is comparatively easy to reckon up the debt of physiology to experiment.

The matter is not at all so simple when we come to practical medicine. Here, experiment is only one out of many factors which have combined to produce a certain result; and if any one chooses to believe that the result would have been produced equally well without experiment, it is impossible to convince him. The fact remains, that it was attained *with* it. It is true that in physiological discoveries also, other processes are used besides experimentation; but it is comparatively easy to assign to each its distinct share. But when the facts thus gained come to be used for the actual practical treatment of sick and suffering human beings, no two of whom are exactly alike, they have to be so cautiously applied, one deduction has to be so qualified by another, individual peculiarities have to be so carefully studied and allowed for, with the constant possibility of some unknown disturbing cause upsetting all calculations, that when success has been attained, it is very hard to say to what it has been due. It would not be strange, therefore, if nothing positive could be said under this heading about experiments on living animals, except that whatever increased physiological knowledge must improve medical practice. If this were all, it would not be a confession of defeat. Suppose that no astronomer were to be allowed to use a sextant, until he could quote some discovery made by its means alone ; or that all thermometers were to be banished from laboratories, unless it could be shown that whatever we know about heat had been learnt from thermometers and nothing else! So with experiment in medicine. It is not the sole instrument of discovery, nor perhaps the most important; but it is an extremely useful instrument,* and in its own place indispensable. Much of its work cannot be disentangled from the general results, and put down to its separate account, but we are not altogether unable to trace its action, and we shall now see what advances in practical medicine can be distinctly ascribed to it.

At every step in an important surgical operation, we are reminded of the discoveries catalogued in the last chapter, and of others flowing out of them.† Perhaps it will be well to quote Ambrose Paré's description of operations in his time, in order to help us to appreciate our privileges. "I observed my masters, whose method I intended to follow, who thought themselves singularly well appointed to stanch a flux of blood, when they were furnished with various store of hot irons and caustic medicines, which they would use to the dismembered part, now one, then another, as they themselves thought meet. Which thing cannot be spoken or but thought upon without great horror, much less acted. For this kind of remedy could not but bring great and tormenting pain to the patient, seeing such fresh wounds made in the quick and sound flesh are endured with exquisite sense. . . . And verily, of such as were

---

* See resolutions of the Medical Congress, held in London in 1881, and of the British Medical Association of same year. Appendix C., ¶ ¶ 4 and 7.

† For answers to objections to this line of argument, see Appendix E., ¶ 2, a.

burnt, the third part scarce ever recovered, and that with much ado, for that combust wounds with difficulty come to cicatrization; for by this burning are caused cruel pains, whence a fever, convulsion, and oft-times other accidents worse than these. Add hereunto, that when the eschar (scale) fell away, oft-times a new hæmorrhage ensued, for stanching whereof they were forced to use other caustic and burning instruments. . . . . Through which occasion the bones were laid bare, whence many were forced, for the remainder of their wretched life, to carry about an ulcer upon that part which was dismembered; which also took away the opportunity of fitting or putting to an artificial leg or arm, instead of that which was taken off."

Compare with this hideous description the processes of a modern amputation. The patient is probably made unconscious by chloroform, which was studied by Simpson in experiments upon the lower animals* as well as on himself and other men. Some other anæsthetic may, however, be used; or, perhaps, some peculiarity in the patient's constitution may make it dangerous to render him insensible. In this case pain may be saved by the sub-cutaneous injection of morphia,† studied by Dr. Alexander Wood and the late Mr. Rynd (of Dublin) upon sporting dogs, and by a committee of the Medical and Chirurgical Society‡ upon other animals. The next step is to empty the limb of blood. Experiment has shown that the blood-vessels have a power of contracting; and they do contract when the pressure is reduced from any cause, such as raising the

* Report of Royal Commission, p. xiii.
† "Sub-cutaneous injection was used in the laboratory for years before it was applied in practice."—*Memorandum of Facts, &c.*, published by the Association for the Advancement of Medicine by Research, p. 11.
‡ *Medico-Chirurgical Transactions*, vol. 51, p. 199.

limb. The surgeon, therefore, holds it up for a time, and it becomes comparatively bloodless. Experiments made by Brown-Séquard and others having taught him how long the tissues can be left completely deprived of blood without risk of mortification, he next ventures to apply Esmarch's elastic bandage, and almost completely empties the limb of the vital fluid.

The cutting being accomplished, the injured arteries are firmly tied before any bleeding occurs, in a fashion which is the result of long discussions and many experiments.* Although the ligature itself is of very old date (definite accounts of it being found in the writings of the Arabians of the tenth and twelfth centuries), yet the right manner of applying it was only arrived at by slow degrees. Up to the beginning of the last century, the nerves used commonly to be tied in, together with the vessels, causing frightful suffering, and frequent death from tetanus. Going, then, into the other extreme, the ligatures used were wide, and they were loosely tied over corks, &c., so as not to injure the coats of the artery; but they failed to stop the bleeding. The experiments of Dr. John Thomson, of Edinburgh, and of Dr. Jones, who followed him, proved that the best method was to tie the artery extremely tightly, which caused the blood within to coagulate, and deposit a clot of solid matter that acted as a stopper to close the opening. As the operator is familiar with the action of the absorbent vessels (discovered by experiment, as related in Chap. VI.), he will use a catgut ligature, which will not need to be pulled away when the wound is healing,† but can be left where it is to

---

* See Appendix E., ¶ 2. *e*.

† It is difficult for any one without experience to realize the annoyance of the old ligatures. Imagine three or four different strings hanging out of one wound for months, sometimes for years, as occurred in the case of Lord Nelson!

be gradually absorbed. And adopting Professor Lister's *aseptic* mode of treatment (chiefly based upon experiment), his ligature—as well as the dressings which he will subsequently use—will be carbolized.*

The amputation itself takes place, perhaps without the shedding of a drop of blood, certainly without the least danger of hæmorrhage. Deaths from this cause—once the surgeon's terror—are now almost unheard of. The wound (kept perfectly clean, and free from all causes of irritation) heals naturally and healthily, with very little pain,—if the aseptic method be employed, with none. There is no fever, no formation of matter, no fear of bleeding coming on from the ends of the cut vessels; and the restorative forces of Nature have full play.

"Look on that picture and on this," and remember that at every step experiment has been the guide from worse to better. The brilliant discovery of Lister was led up to by the experimental researches into wound-fever carried on by Lee, Bennett, Pasteur, Colin, Toussaint, Weber, Breuer and Chroback, and Koch. They investigated and experimented, finding out gradually what the fever was *not*, and what did *not* cause it; then what it was, and what *did* cause it; and thus they prepared the field for the original genius that struck out the method of prevention. And if any be inclined to object that hundreds of animals were sacrificed in the process of discovery, let him think of the thousands of men who have been sacrificed for want of it, and who would in all future ages—as long as man is liable to disease or injury, and particularly so long as war lasts—have died miserably in festering hospitals of all the horrible varieties of simple or secondary wound-fever, and the other consequences of wound-infection. The perfecting of this mode of treatment has now been forbidden by the

* See Appendix, E., ¶ 2, γ.

Home Secretary; but enough had been done before the reign of "Zoophilism" in England to secure a great saving in human life, and the good work is being carried on in other countries.

Until within the present century, surgeons used to divide one of the nerves of the face (the *portio dura* of the seventh pair), in hopes of curing neuralgia. But as the nerve had nothing whatever to do with sensation, the only result was to destroy motion in that side of the face. The experiments which revealed the true functions of the nerve, at last put an end to this piece of stupidity. This same nerve often loses its power of action from one of many various causes affecting different portions of it; and the treatment must be different according to the part affected. This can only be discovered from indications, the meaning of which has been learnt from vivisections, in combination, of course, with anatomy.

If a man has fallen into the water, and become insensible before he is taken out,—or fallen down an old well, or in any other way has had his blood poisoned with carbonic acid gas (which we call being suffocated), the best means to restore him is artificial respiration. But here we are again indebted to experiment on living animals; for this method was used upon them by Vesalius, Hooke, Lower, and others, long before it was applied to the resuscitation of human beings.

Suppose, however, that he has been suffocated by the fumes of charcoal; if the mischief has gone far, artificial respiration will not bring him round. We may go on trying it until all hope is lost, if we do not know what Claude Bernard's experiments have proved,—that the carbonic oxide gas given off by burning charcoal makes a more stable compound with the colouring matter of the blood, which prevents it henceforward from uniting with oxygen.

So that it is useless to pump in supplies of fresh air; the only thing to be done is to get rid at once of the spoiled blood, and replace it with new. This can be done by transfusion, or injecting enough blood from a healthy person to keep the system alive until it can produce more for itself. In the same way, when life is all but lost from hæmorrhage, it can be recalled by a fresh supply of the vital fluid. It is only from repeated and careful experiments that surgeons have learnt how to perform this operation with success. It is never done except as a last resource, when everything else has failed; and so far has saved more than half the cases in which it has been attempted.*

Great improvements in orthopædic surgery are due to the physiological investigations of Stromeyer, Von Ammon, Bouvier, Guérin, and others, in the present century.

Tenotomy (or the surgery of tendons) has only been carried on in a scientific manner and with successful results since the subcutaneous method of performing the operation was perfected, and the repair of tendons investigated on the lower animals by the same experimenters.†

The possibility of operating with the knife upon the stomach and intestines was only proved by experiments upon animals, especially by the easy establishment of gastric fistulæ in dogs. In the same manner, the methods of operation were studied; and, consequently, diseases which were formerly considered hopeless are now brought within reach of amelioration or cure.‡

It sometimes happens that tumours are situated either where they cannot be reached by the knife, or where the hæmorrhage when they are removed cannot be arrested. In such a case, nothing could be done for the patient until the invention of M. Chassaignac's *écraseur*, an instrument

* See Appendix E., ¶ 2, ι.
† See Appendix E., ¶ 2, η.
‡ Heidenhain, loc. cit., p. 37.

which slowly tears through the tissue instead of cutting it. In this way, there is almost no bleeding, and the operation can be performed with safety. It was necessary, however, that he should test his instrument before using it on human beings; and he satisfied himself of its value and safety by experiments upon dogs, instead of upon hospital patients.

No one would have supposed that a creature could live in perfect health with only one kidney, when Nature has supplied it with two, until the fact had been proved upon dogs. This knowledge has emboldened surgeons to attempt the operation of removal in human cases; it has now frequently been performed, and repeatedly been successful, where all other means of prolonging life or making it bearable had failed.

Billroth, the celebrated Vienna surgeon, had a patient who was threatened with sudden death from malignant disease of the larynx. The only hope that he could see lay in removing the entire organ; but the operation had never been performed before, and he could not venture to attempt it for the first time upon a man. His assistant, Czerny, however, performed it successfully upon several dogs; and by using his experience, Billroth was able to save his patient's life. The man recovered, and with an artificial larynx was able to breathe, and even to speak in a whisper.*

In some very bad cases of injury to the skin, especially from extensive burns or scalds, when it has been completely destroyed over a large surface—the patient would die of exhaustion, before the cuticle could renew itself by the slow process of growth from the edges inwards. But in consequence of experiments in animal grafting (as it is called), pieces of cuticle can now be removed from other parts of the body and *planted* on the denuded surface, where they

* Heidenhain, loc. cit., p. 39.

will, as it were, take root from, and cover it over. On a similar principle artificial noses are made, and a hideous disfigurement is changed into a very tolerable ugliness.

These are some of the most distinctly quotable cases in which improvements in treatment can be directly traced to experiments upon living animals. But as improved treatment must almost necessarily follow upon increased knowledge of the disease, those series of experiments which have taught us more of the processes of illness find their place in this chapter. So many different experimenters have contributed to the advancement of this department of pathology that it would be impossible to name all and invidious to name some,—especially as a discovery has often resulted from the work of one man combined with that of another, and cannot justly be assigned to any individual. It will be best simply to mention some of the most valuable additions to our knowledge of this subject which we owe to experiment upon living animals.

In few departments of medicine is there a greater advance to look back upon, and to look forward to—than in the treatment of fever. An accurate knowledge of the manner in which it kills its victims is being attained by means of experiments upon animals,[*] and there is every reason to

[*] These are the celebrated "baking alive" experiments. The term is an especial favourite, being a peculiarly unpleasant one, and it would also convey to most minds the false impression that the animals are put into a *hot* oven. The fact is that the temperature of their blood is gradually raised by heat, until they die,—exactly as our blood would be raised by fever, until we died. The symptoms are the quickening of the breathing and the pulse, and then the gasping and panting with which the watchers by sick-beds are only too painfully familiar, but which cannot be described as acute suffering. Finally, the animal falls into convulsions, *when it becomes unconscious*, and any sound which it may make denotes no pain. The process now usually lasts for about two hours. Bernard, in these experiments, used two pigeons, two guinea-pigs, less than twenty rabbits, and six dogs. (Sir William Gull in *Nineteenth Century*

expect that this knowledge will also supply the means of saving them.

There are two forms of dropsy, one arising from disorder of the nervous system, and the other from derangement of the secretions. Until experiments upon the mechanism of the circulation, and the effects of the nervous system on it, enabled physicians to distinguish between the two, they used to be treated alike, often with fatal results.

Apoplexy is often caused by a clot which has formed in the blood, and stops up one of the vessels of the brain, thus preventing that part from obtaining its usual nourishment of blood. Before this was understood, an apoplectic patient used to be bled, and robbed of a quantity of the very blood for which his brain was starving. Experiments on the effect of plugging arteries (embolism) made this clear, and explained other obscure cases of sudden death: and apoplexy is now treated in a more rational and successful manner.

Formerly, if a bone was found to be diseased, there was nothing to be done but to amputate the limb to which it belonged. But experiments on the mode of repair of fractured or injured bone, particularly those of Duhamel (1740), Sir Astley Cooper (1820), and Syme (1831),—have now led surgeons to content themselves with removing the diseased portion of bone, carefully leaving the membrane which surrounded it to produce (as it will in time) a tolerable substitute. In this way, a healthy hand may now be left

---

for March, 1882, p. 460.) A medical opponent replies to this, that zymotic diseases cannot be cured by medicine, though they can be prevented by hygiene. If they cannot be directly cured by medicine, they can certainly be alleviated and controlled by treatment; and how can either treatment or prevention be thoroughly carried out, except with a thorough knowledge of the nature and causes of the disease in question? Are we to understand that he declines to treat fever cases, considering that "drugs are impotent?" (See Appendix E.)

at the extremity of an arm which has lost a piece of its bone, instead of an unsightly and comparatively useless stump.

Redfern, Cohnheim, von Recklinghausen, and others have conducted experiments into the nature and origin of inflammation, by which knowledge has been gained that is of use almost at every turn in treatment. It is not necessary to dwell on the importance of understanding the most widespread of all diseased symptoms.

Another way in which experiments upon living creatures have contributed to improvements in treatment, is by the testing of various drugs, whose effects are tried upon the lower animals, in order to judge of their probable value or uselessness to man. It is quite true that positive conclusions cannot be drawn in this way. All drugs do not affect all animals alike, any more than they do all men. Rabbits can eat belladonna, and be none the worse for it; while it is dangerous to give chloroform to dogs, though most men and women can take it safely. But these notable exceptions are noted *because* they are exceptions: on the whole, a substance which will poison a cat will not agree with a dog, and what will excite the heart of a frog is likely to do the same to a man. In short, the effect of a drug upon one of the lower animals furnishes a strong presumption— though not an infallible indication—of what its effect will be upon a human being. And in such a hazardous proceeding as that of introducing a new substance into the complex human economy, it is surely necessary that there should be at least a strong presumption that it will do good, and not harm. But this could never be gained without experiment; and by means of experiment it often has been gained, with the result of adding many new and valuable remedies to the pharmacopœia. In this way *chloral hydrate* was discovered; and the fact that it has been sometimes misused does not make it the less soothing and useful when properly administered. The use of *atropin* to check the flow of saliva was thus learnt, and great relief can now be given to a most distressing feature in some cases of paralysis and fracture of the skull. The manner in which *belladonna* acts as a poison has been shown by experiments; and so also has it been proved that a substance extracted from *calabar bean* is its antidote. The stimulating effects of *strychnia* upon the spinal cord were made out by Magendie's experiments; by the same means it was tested for practice, and established as a valuable nerve tonic; and by the same means also, Professor Haughton introduced *nicotin* as its antidote. Very little could be done for the agonizing disease called angina pectoris, until it was discovered that *nitrite of amyl* causes general relaxation of the blood-vessels, which in that complaint are believed to be in a state of spasm; and it has proved a most valuable remedy. Every new drug introduced into the pharmacopœia up to the passing of the "Cruelty to Animals" Act, 1876, might in fact be added to the list; but these are the most salient instances, and they will be valuable for the guidance of those persons who say they are determined not to avail themselves of the benefits of experiment. They now know a few of the remedies they should avoid, in case of meeting with untoward accidents in the way of poisons and diseases; and it will perhaps be kinder to increase their chances of life by not mentioning more.

Besides the effect of experiment upon direct treatment, it has had an important influence upon preventive medicine. The investigations which have taught us the origin and processes of many diseases, both of animals and man—though they may not have supplied modes of cure—have erected finger-posts pointing out what to avoid, and what sources of disease to eliminate; and, though it is a good thing to know how to cure a disease when you have got it, it is a much better thing to know how to keep from getting it. Thus, it is of great importance to have learnt from experiment that cholera is chiefly communicated by drinking water, and that consumption is infective. The aseptic treatment already referred to is based upon researches of this class, and so is the method of preventive inoculation. This has been greatly ridiculed by writers who have affected to suppose that all sorts of disgusting diseases were to be given to animals and men, in order to prevent their catching them! Any treatment can be reduced to an absurdity, if it is supposed to be used without common sense or discretion; but sharp weapons are for skilled hands. Preventive inoculation would only be used where there was sufficient danger of contracting the actual disease to make it worth while to produce the milder type. In small-pox such a danger is constant; in animal epidemics, and probably some human maladies, the occasions for using this preventive arise from time to time, as a wave of infection swells towards us. By this and other means the sources of silkworm disease, small-pox of sheep, cattle plague, splenic fever, farcy, glanders, and anthrax (both among sheep and men), can now be grappled with, and degrees of success attained, varying from perfect immunity to useful alleviations.* All the progress hitherto made in this direction is, of course, due to experiments upon animals of the class concerned; all the progress to be made in future depends upon whether these experiments are continued or stopped.

The part of experiment in the progress of medicine is not confined to such results as can be catalogued. At every turn it controls observations, corrects deductions, verifies

* See Appendix C. Section II.

discoveries, tests improvements, suggests inquiries, always (as Professor Sharpey so well said before the Royal Commission) "putting a lamp in the hand of the physician." This lamp has been turned down rather low in England, but it still burns. Will the world be the better if it is altogether extinguished, and the task of shedding light upon the onward path of medicine left to the torch-bearers of other countries? For it is inevitable that—if the present anti-experimental agitation should prove successful—its history must tend to force all physiologists into identifying tenderness to animals with unscientific sentimentalism, and unreasoning disregard of the sufferings of men. And that injury to their finer feelings which is now supposed to have resulted from the free exercise of their profession, must in truth come to pass in some measure from its enslavement in England.

CHAPTER VIII.

LEGISLATION: PAST, PRESENT, AND POSSIBLE.

General state of the law—Martin's Act—No English physiologist prosecuted under it—The "Hand-book to the Physiological Laboratory"—The Norwich experiment — Appointment of the Royal Commission—Its conclusions from the evidence—Recommendations—The Act of 1876—Its principal provisions—Defects—Autocracy of the Home Secretary—Mode of proceeding under the Act—Action of the Home Secretary—Bill for the Total Abolition of Vivisection—Desirable modifications in the working of the Act—Responsibility to be left to the signatories—Certificates unnecessary for inoculations—Licenses held by medical instructors to hold good for their term of office—What is abstractly desirable.

EVERY one may not be acquainted with the exact state of the law at present, as regards cruelty to animals, and scientific experiments. It is very curious and interesting, and has the great merit of being peculiarly British. That is to say, it is not trammelled by any principle previously laid down, or hindered by any consideration of reasoning or consistency. To found a new law upon a distinct principle, from which its enactments develop logically, has a Continental flavour about it displeasing to the national mind, and reminds us in some way of centralization. We prefer to make a fresh regulation every now and then, when it occurs to us, or when somebody makes a fuss, and it is necessary to do something. In this way a state of things has come about, in which it is penal to use domestic animals in any way cruelly, but in which any one may torture wild creatures in whatever fashion he likes, *provided it be not for scientific purposes;* while any invertebrate animal is given up to whatever any one chooses to inflict, for any or no reason. The older law against cruelty to animals, commonly known as Martin's Act, applies only to those which we call domestic. It did not therefore need the Act of 1876 to protect horses, asses, and mules, cats and dogs, from cruelty; while, now that it has been passed, an otter may be killed by inches to amuse a crowd of men, or boys may roast a rabbit to death for fun; but if there be a serious scientific reason for giving pain to a rat, the operator is a criminal, unless he is shielded by a fence of licenses and certificates. Thus, Mary Ann, the housemaid, may kill all the mice in the house with the horrible poison of phosphorus, and no one will interfere with her; but if Mary Ann's master, the surgeon, injects snake-poison into one of them in hopes of discovering an antidote for it, he becomes liable to a £50 fine. And if Mary Ann, being tender-hearted, and disliking smells behind the wainscoting, has recourse to live traps, and is then puzzled to know how to dispose of her prey, she may give it to the stable-boy to amuse his terrier with, but she must not give it to the surgeon to experiment on. Nothing makes it criminal to give pain to a wild animal, *except* having sufficient justification. In a new sense, *qui s'excuse s'accuse.* Briefly, the case stands thus: You must have a good reason for hurting a tame creature; you must *not* have a good reason for hurting a wild creature; and you need have no reason at all for hurting an invertebrate creature.

Before physiologists and invertebrates had been thus unfavourably distinguished from their fellow creatures, Martin's Act was the only law upon this subject; but it was amply sufficient to protect domestic animals from anything that could be really called cruelty. The Royal Society for the Prevention of Cruelty to Animals exists for the very purpose of prosecuting such acts. As we find it later on proposing legislation for the purpose of restricting experiment, we naturally expect to find that it first exhausted the powers of the existing law. We expect to learn that its numerous prosecutions against those who "tortured" cats and dogs failed to repress the odious practice, either because it was so widespread as to be irrepressible, or because the sentences which could be imposed under Martin's Act were not sufficiently severe. But it is not so. We look vainly for the prosecutions, vainly for the sentences, most vainly of all for the evidence of "tortures" needlessly inflicted by any English physiologist. The S. P. C. A. itself tells us* that they have employed "the surveillance of detectives, and vigorously pursued the prosecution of offenders;" but we learn from the same authority that "the only prosecution ever instituted against vivisectors under a penal statute [was] the celebrated Norwich proceedings." After all, detectives and vigour are not all that is needed for an action at law; there must also be something to be detected. Up to the sitting of the Royal Commission in 1875, evidence had not been forthcoming to bring a charge of cruelty to animals home to any English physiologist. The Society attributes this to the difficulty of obtaining entrance to laboratories, or evidence of what goes on there. But the laboratories at Westminster Hospital, St. Bartholomew's Hospital, Guy's Hospital, the Brown Institution, and St. George's Hospital, were opened to its agents when they applied for admission (a privilege of which they seem only to have availed themselves in two cases out of the five); and considering the large number of

* *Vivisection*, Introduction, p. 5. Published for the Royal Society for the Prevention of Cruelty to Animals.

students and servants who must be privy to whatever horrors are supposed to go on in other laboratories, it is incredible that no evidence could have been forthcoming in any single case, if cruelty had really been practised to an extent calling for special legislation. Whatever explanation may be put forward, these are the plain facts—that the Society never instituted a prosecution for cruelty to animals against one of the English physiologists, and that—both in the temperate statement above quoted, and in the evidence before the Royal Commission of the Secretary, Mr. Colam (already referred to)—it was admitted that, as a general rule, they used anæsthetics wherever possible consistently with the experiment, and could not be convicted of a single case of wanton cruelty.

Matters stood thus previous to the meeting of the British Medical Association at Norwich in 1874. Considerable feeling had been excited in the lay public by a work written by Drs. J. Burdon Sanderson and Michael Foster, entitled "Handbook to the Physiological Laboratory," and published in 1871. This book was intended for "beginners" in experimental physiology (who must necessarily be advanced students in the ordinary science of medicine); it was meant to be used under supervision in a regular laboratory; the use of anæsthetics was taken for granted, just as it would be in a book on operative surgery; and descriptions were inserted of experiments which had been made, but which it would not be necessary to repeat. When such a work was read by excited and sensitive lay men and women, ignorant of qualifications which would be obvious to the people for whom it was intended—they leaped to the conclusion that raw medical students were being encouraged to repeat for their pleasure every experiment that had ever yielded results, careless whether the subjects were conscious or unconscious of pain. This misconception did a great deal to raise the temperature of popular feeling. At this time, then, an "Anti-Vivisection" agitation was in the air, but it had not gathered to a point; the vigilant S. P. C. A. had its detectives at work, but had detected nothing; and physiologists were going on with their business, unlicensed and unlibelled. Then occurred the Norwich incident, when Dr. Magnan injected absinthe into the veins of one dog, with the effect of producing epileptic convulsions,—and alcohol into those of another, with the effect of making it drunk. The object was to show the different action of the two drugs, in order to enable doctors to diagnose their use, and to show the dangers of absinthe drinking. The S. P. C. A. now instituted their first prosecution, but it was not a successful one. Dr. Magnan was beyond the jurisdiction of English courts, and the English doctors who were arraigned with him could not be proved to have taken any part in the experiment. The public mind, however, was highly excited; and the agitation, which had been simmering, rose, and boiled over into the newspapers. Letters appeared, describing proceedings in foreign laboratories, in which the experiments were dwelt upon in painful detail, and nothing was said about their objects, which were probably not known to the writers. And it was concluded that everything which had been done in Florence or Paris was, or would be, repeated in London, because one dog had been made epileptic and another drunk, in the presence of a body of scientific men.

Many persons who thoroughly appreciated the value of experiment upon living animals, yet felt that it was a practice liable to abuse, and needing to be guarded by certain restrictions; the medical profession, as a whole, had a clear conscience, and courted investigation; and therefore no opposition was made to the appointment of a Royal Commission to inquire into the matter. This Commission was appointed in June 1875, and reported on January 8, 1876. It consisted of Viscount Cardwell, Baron Winmarleigh, the Right Honourable W. E. Forster, Sir John Burgess Karslake, Professor Huxley, Mr. Erichsen, and Mr. Hutton (editor of the *Spectator*). After having examined a large number of medical and other witnesses, and received all the evidence that was laid before them by the Societies for the Prevention of Cruelty to Animals, and the Total Abolition of Vivisection, the Commission arrived at the following conclusions:

The number of persons systematically engaged in the performance of experiments upon living animals did not exceed 15 or 20. (Report, page viii.) A general sentiment of humanity on this subject appeared to pervade all classes in this country, not excepting medical students, physiologists, and scientific men in general. (*Ibid.*, p. x.) The evidence of medical instructors was unanimous to the effect that students would not tolerate the performance of cruel demonstrations before them.* It would require a voluminous treatise to exhibit in a consecutive statement the benefits that medicine and surgery have derived from the discoveries of the circulation of the blood, the lacteal and lymphatic system of vessels, and the compound function of the spinal nerves, made by experiments on living animals. (*Ibid.*, p. xiii.) "It is not possible for us to recommend that the Indian Government should be prohibited from pursuing its endeavours [by experiment] to discover an antidote for snake-bites; or that, without such an effort, your Majesty's Indian subjects should be left to perish in large numbers annually from the effects of these poisons; nor can we say that new medicinal agents ought, in the

* See Appendix A, ¶¶ 7 and 8.

first instance, to be tried upon man, when the risk to human life might have been prevented by a previous trial on animals. We cannot recommend that criminals like Palmer should be permitted to escape, or persons suspected be deprived of the means of establishing their innocence." (*Ibid.*, p. xiv.) "We cannot recommend the total prohibition of experiments of [the inoculatory] class." (*Ibid.* p. xv.)

In short, to quote Lord Sherbrooke (then the Right Hon. Robert Lowe), "the Commission entirely acquitted English physiologists of the charge of cruelty. They pronounced a well-merited eulogium on the humanity of the medical profession in England. They pointed out that medical students were extremely sensitive to the infliction of pain upon animals, and that the feeling of the public at large was penetrated by the same sentiment. They then proceeded to consider to what restrictions they should subject the humane and excellent persons in whose favour they had so decidedly reported. Their proceeding was very singular. They acquitted the accused, and sentenced them to be under the surveillance of the police for life."*

When the Commission arrived at the practical part of their report, they declared it to be impossible to abolish all experiments on living animals, impossible to limit it to the "immediate application of an expected discovery to some prophylactic or therapeutic end," and undesirable to forbid all such demonstrations to students. But they advised that the latter should only be exhibited with anæsthetics (in which they only repeated a resolution passed by the Physiological section of the British Association in 1871,† and approved by the leading scientific and medical men of the day); and their chief recommendation was that the whole matter of

* *Contemporary Review*, October, 1876.
† See Appendix A, ¶ 9.

making experiments upon living animals should be placed under the control of the Secretary of State, who should have power to grant and withdraw licenses for their performance. The holders of licenses should be bound by conditions, the breach of which should render the license liable to forfeiture ; and the general scope of these conditions should be " to ensure that suffering should never be inflicted in any case in which it could be avoided, and should be reduced to a minimum where it could not be altogether avoided. In the administration of the system generally, the responsible minister would of course be guided by the opinion of advisers of competent knowledge and experience, selected by himself, whose names should be made known to the profession and the public. The appointment of an inspector or inspectors will be necessary, (who) must be persons of such character and position as to command the confidence of the public no less than that of men of science. The holder of a license, when he receives notice that the Secretary of State intends to withdraw it during the period for which it has been granted, should be at liberty to demand a public enquiry," and if successful, might be allowed " the reasonable costs of his defence." (*Report*, pp. xxii. and xxiii.)*

Mr. Hutton, who takes a prominent part in opposing experiments on living animals, and who throughout the inquiry acted as examining counsel for the " Anti-Vivisectionists," appended to this report one of his own, in which he urged that dogs and cats should be altogether exempted from experiment of this kind. But as he expressed no dissent from the principles of the joint report, which he signed, it appears that—however strongly prejudiced an intelligent person may be on the anti-scientific side of the question—he finds it impossible (when brought

* See Appendix F, ¶ 2.

face to face with the evidence) to deny the necessity of such experiments to physiology, medicine, and surgery, or to recommend its total abolition.

In the course of the same year (1876), an Act was passed through Parliament, based upon the report of the Commission, but departing from it in some important particulars. The following is a summary of its principal provisions.

§ 2. A person shall not perform or take part in performing on a living animal any experiment calculated to give pain, except subject to the restrictions imposed by this Act; under a penalty not exceeding £50 for the first offence, and for the second, or any subsequent offence, a penalty not exceeding £100, or imprisonment for a period not exceeding three months.   § 3. A permissible experiment "must be performed with a view to the advancement by new discovery of physiological knowledge, or of knowledge which will be useful for saving or prolonging life or alleviating suffering," by a person holding such a licence as is subsequently prescribed. The animal must during the whole of the experiment be under some anæsthetic of sufficient power to prevent its feeling pain ; and if the pain is likely to continue after the effect of the anæsthetic has ceased, or if any serious injury has been inflicted upon the animal, it must be killed before it recovers from the influence of the anæsthetic. The experiment shall not be performed as an illustration of lectures in medical schools, hospitals, colleges, or elsewhere, or for the purpose of attaining manual skill. The following exceptions are made : Experiments may be performed as illustrations to lectures, if anæsthetics are used, *and* if a certificate, as subsequently described, be given that the proposed experiments are absolutely necessary for the due instruction of the persons to whom such lectures are delivered—with a view to their acquiring physiological knowledge, or knowledge which will be useful to them for saving or prolonging life, or alleviating suffering; anæsthetics—in experiments for purposes of discovery—may be dispensed with under a certificate that their use would frustrate the purposes of the experiment; the animal need not be killed before recovery from the anæsthetic, if it is certified that its death would frustrate the object of the experiment, provided it be killed as soon as such object has been attained;* and experiments may be performed in order to test a previous discovery alleged to have been made for the advancement of physiological knowledge, &c., under certificate that such testing is absolutely necessary for the advancement of such knowledge. § 4. Curare is not recognized as an anæsthetic. § 5. Painful experiments are not to be performed upon horses, asses, or mules—or upon dogs or cats without anæsthetics—except with a special certificate that no other animal is suitable and available for the experiment. § 6. All exhibitions of experiments to the general public are illegal, and subject any one taking any part in promoting them to a penalty. § 7. All experiments performed for the purpose of instruction shall be carried out in a registered place; and the Secretary of State, when granting the license for any experiment, may insert in the license a provision that it shall be performed in a registered place. § 8. The Secretary of State may grant this license to "any person whom he may think qualified," "for such time as he may think fit"; and it may be revoked by him on his being satisfied that such license ought to be revoked. There may be annexed to such license any conditions which the Secretary of State may think expedient for the purpose of better carrying into effect the objects of this Act, but not

---

* If the object of the experiment were to study a mode of treatment for some disease, or the best method of performing some operation,— the animal would (according to this section) have to be killed as soon as it was obviously recovering.

inconsistent with the provisions thereof. § 9. He may direct any person performing experiments under this Act, from time to time, to make such reports to him of the result of such experiments, in such form and with such details as he may require. § 10. All registered places shall be visited by inspectors appointed by him. § 11. Any application for a license under this Act, and all the certificates above referred to, must be signed by one or more of the presidents of the Royal Society, the Royal Society of Edinburgh, the Royal Irish Academy, the Royal Colleges of Surgeons in London, Edinburgh, or Dublin, the Royal Colleges of Physicians in the same cities, the General Medical Council, and the Faculty of Physicians and Surgeons of Glasgow (and in the case of veterinary experiments, by the president of the Royal College of Veterinary Surgeons, or of the Royal Veterinary College, London); and also by a professor of physiology, medicine, anatomy, medical jurisprudence, materia medica, or surgery, in a university in Great Britain or Ireland, or in University College, London, or in a chartered college in Great Britain or Ireland, unless the applicant be himself such a professor. If he be one of the presidents named, however, he will still require the signature of another president. A certificate may be given by the persons specified for any time or any series of experiments *they* may think fit. A copy of any certificate under this section shall be forwarded to the Secretary of State, but shall not be available for a week afterwards; and the Secretary of State may at any time disallow or suspend it. § 12. The powers conferred by this Act of granting a license or giving a certificate may be exercised by an order in writing under the hand of any judge (as specified), when he is satisfied that it is essential for the purposes of justice in a criminal case to make such experiment. §§ 18 to 19 specify the manner, &c., of legal proceedings. § 20. In the application of this Act to Ireland, the term "Secretary of State" shall be construed to mean the Chief Secretary to the Lord Lieutenant for the time being. § 21. A prosecution under this Act *against a licensed person* shall not be instituted except with the assent in writing of the Secretary of State. § 22. This Act shall not apply to invertebrate animals.

The persons in the Act who correspond to the "competent advisers," by whom the Commissioners advised that the Secretary of State should be guided, are evidently the eminent men who are empowered to recommend the issue of licenses and to grant certificates; and it would certainly seem to be the intention of the Act that they should be the judges of the matter, and that the Secretary should be ruled by their opinion. But if so, it is very faultily expressed, as it actually leaves him at liberty entirely to disregard their advice. Also, there is no provision made for appeal on the part of a licensee who may consider himself aggrieved by the withdrawal of his license. In these two respects, the legislation now in force is much more unfavourable to experimental physiologists than that recommended by the Royal Commissioners.

When we come to investigate what is theoretically permitted by this remarkable Act, we find that the principle which I have laid down in Chapters III. and IV. is (after all) tacitly conceded in clause 3; for it is there enacted that (upon the recommendation of certain specified persons, and with the consent of the Secretary of State) an experiment may be performed, and performed without anæsthetics— provided that it be for the advancement or testing of physiological knowledge, or of knowledge which will be useful for saving or prolonging life, or alleviating suffering, and that anæsthetics are inadmissible in the case. Now here is the very point. Physiologists do not wish to perform experiments for any other object except the advance of physiological and medical knowledge; they are perfectly ready and willing to use anæsthetics whenever possible; they can, therefore, have no objection to this clause, as a matter of principle. But it is a very important practical question: Who is to be the judge of what experiments will promote such knowledge? The Commissioners say the Secretary of State, *guided by competent advisers*. In practice, it is the Secretary of State of his own knowledge and wisdom.

The result of placing an uncontrolled discretion in the hands of one man is that the effect of the law in question depends almost entirely upon the manner in which it is administered. In fact, it is plain that—for the regulating of experiments—the State is the Home Secretary. He could, if he chose, as a matter of course, grant every license, and disallow no certificate—thus leaving the real power to the heads of the medical and surgical authorities nominated in the Act; or he could refuse every application, and practically carry out the views of the extremest anti-vivisectionists. No one can interfere with him, and he is responsible to no one. The law means as much or as little as he chooses to make it mean; but this it always means with no uncertainty—that a layman selected for his political views, and his qualifications for revising sentences, keeping Local Boards in order, attending to every one's grievances, and generally doing the odd jobs of the nation—is appointed Dictator over the Medical Profession. He, in the last resort, is the supreme judge as to whether a certain experiment will or will not promote physiological knowledge, or whether it will do so in a degree sufficient to justify the infliction of pain.

A man ignorant of medicine—or even whose medical knowledge has not been duly tested and certified—is punished if he prescribes physic, and attempts to cure other men; but the same ignorance—if he only be Home Secretary—need not prevent his stopping the researches of other men, when they are seeking fresh modes of cure. It is no new experience in the world—that knowledge is needed to do good, but none to hinder it; still, it seems strange to find the fact embodied as a principle of an English law. The chief fault, therefore, of the Act of 1876 is that *it lays in the hands of a single and irresponsible man a power requiring skilled knowledge in its use, without making any provision that he shall be qualified to exercise it.* Let us now inquire in what manner it has been exercised.

The actual mode of proceeding under the Act is this. If a medical man is engaged in any inquiry requiring him to make an experiment upon a living animal, for which it is likely to be any the worse afterwards (say, to be blind or deaf, or to have some kind of disease), and to keep it alive to watch the effect—he finds that it is first necessary to purchase a printed form of application for license, from Messrs. Churchill and Co., New Burlington-street. Having filled this up duly, he must get the signatures beforementioned, and then send it in to the Home Secretary. After waiting about three weeks, he may get his license, or he may not. If he gets it, he must then go about getting his certificate, have it also signed, and forward it. According to the Act, if he received no answer to the contrary within a week, he would be at liberty to act upon it; but a negative answer is always sent at once, that the Home Secretary may be on the safe side, and he then takes his time to think over the matter. Perhaps in about another three weeks, the applicant may receive the permission which the Secretary of State's "competent advisers" have already long since granted to him; but if he has had inoculatory matter or disease-germs waiting all the time, he has probably ceased to concern himself greatly about the result.

Although very few applications for a license have been ultimately refused, yet such applications have been refused at first, and certificates disallowed; and they have only subsequently been granted or allowed after long delay, and by the help of strong pressure upon the Home Office. Some certificates have been absolutely disallowed, and in several cases experiments have been prevented by intimations that application would be useless. Up to December, 1881, seven certificates had been disallowed; a delay, which defeated the object of the application, and amounted to practical refusal, took place in six cases; and in five the applicant was deterred from making a formal request.* In this manner, the Medical Dictator has prevented researches into antidotes to snake poisons, the multiplication of septic organisms,† the physiology of the brain, the functions of the spleen, the method of renal secretion, aseptic dressing of wounds, the actions of certain poisons, intestinal secretion and movements, ligatures on arteries, and other matters. To such a simple practical issue has the matter been brought, that men are left to die of poison, wounds, and disease, for want of the knowledge that can only be obtained at the expense of animals. And the course adopted by the Home Secretary is the more striking, because one of these very classes of experiments (that on snake bites) is instanced by the Royal Commissioners as an argument against the entire prohibition of what is called Vivisection. Thus the very investigation whose importance was considered by them to be a *raison*

* *Memorandum* of the Physiological Society, 1881.

† The microscopic vegetable growths which give rise to putrefaction in all its forms, and therefore to the inflammation of wounds, and many diseases.

d'être for experiment on living animals—has been simply prohibited by the executive authority. In a controversy where strong language has so much abounded, it is best to restrain indignation, yet it is difficult to write coolly of this deliberate shortening of the hand stretched out to save life. Just as Dr. Brunton has been forbidden to seek for antidotes to snake-bites, so has Professor Fraser been checked in his attempts to study the nature of the poison used by the natives of Borneo upon their arrows, in hopes of providing some safeguard for the English colonists now moving in that direction; while Professor Lister has had to leave England in order to carry on his researches. And besides the list of stifled investigations already given, how many more are left unattempted because of the difficulties thrown in the way ? And in the face of all this knowledge already refused, and help and healing shut away from suffering men, we are threatened in the name of religion and humanity with a still further curtailing of the working powers of physiology! ONE spoke long ago in the name of religion and humanity as no other can claim to speak after Him; but what He said must sound out of tune to our modern "Zoophilists." For, as has been quoted by Prof. Yeo,* His estimate was: "Ye are of more value than many sparrows ;"† and it was in conclusive certainty that he asked: "Is not a man better than a sheep ?"‡

If the whole state of the law about cruelty to animals is anomalous, and that part of it which controls scientific experiment was unjustly framed, and is harshly administered, what is now to be recommended ? We know of one simple and sweeping proposal, that of the Bill intro-

* *Fortnightly Review*, March, 1882, p. 366.
† St. Luke, xii., 7.
‡ St. Matthew, xii., 12.

duced into the House of Commons in February, 1882, by Mr. Reid, Sir Eardley Wilmot, Mr. Samuel Morley, and Mr. Firth, and known as "The Vivisection Abolition Bill." If that Bill should become law, it will not be lawful to subject any animal to vivisection, that is to say, " to perform on any live animal, with or without the use of anæsthetics, any experiment or demonstration for any medical, physiological, or scientific purpose." (Clause 2.) It is only fair to say that in general the supporters of this measure propose, when they have abolished hurting animals for the sake of knowledge, to consider if they cannot attempt to abolish hurting them for the sake of amusement. As the British public is keenly alive to the benefits of sport, but not so sensitive to those of science, the second task would probably be harder than the first. But it is to be hoped that the same public has still enough common sense left to render even the destruction of experimental physiology no easy work.

On the other hand, the defenders of Medical Research ask for no such sweeping measure on their side. They have not demanded the repeal of the Act 39 and 40 Vict. ch. 77, whose short and insulting title is " The Cruelty to Animals Act, 1876." They would be content if it were administered in a spirit which takes for granted more humanity in experimenters, less omniscience in Home Secretaries, and more trustworthiness in their advisers—than the present system implies. The Royal Commissioners—we know—presumed that the Dictator would be guided by "competent advisers;" and the Act provided them for him, in the persons of the heads of the medical and surgical professions, who have the power of certifying that a certain person is a suitable one to hold a license, that a certain experiment is necessary for instruction, cannot be performed without anæsthetics, requires the keeping alive of the animal after it is concluded, or is necessary for testing a previous discovery. It is surely absurd that an unqualified person should have the power of going behind the opinions of these high authorities, and contradicting them upon their own ground. On the contrary, the Home Secretary's professional advisers ought to be, like the Queen's, responsible for all technical points; and licenses ought to be granted and certificates allowed, as a matter of course, to properly recommended applicants. In cases of abuse, he will always have the power of withdrawing the license,—a power which ought to be exercised—not autocratically, but (as advised by the Royal Commissioners) after a formal investigation. In fact, the Act is at present worked on the principle that medical men are not to be trusted, their leaders' certificates not to be depended upon, and that cruelty would be the rule, if it were not made impossible. But the profession was tried for cruelty before the Royal Commission, and was acquitted. It would only be fair, therefore, to act on the basis of that acquittal, and admit that abuse of their very restricted liberty is to be looked for as the exception and not the rule. Therefore let the determination of who is to be licensed, and for what, rest with those who understand the subject-matter of the decision. They are the best judges of the value of what is proposed to be done, and the sense of responsibility to the nation, and the public opinion of their own profession, will be amply sufficient safeguards against too great laxity. Probably the members of the "anti-vivisectionist" societies do not believe that there is any such professional public opinion; but there is, and it is an effectual, though quiet check on the few who need it. *But if any influence from outside could injure it, it would be the constant ignoring and denying of its existence.* It is not generally found an incentive to honesty to tell a man, "You would be a thief if you could, and therefore I shall keep all my goods under lock and key when you are about, and have my eye on you when you don't expect it." Weak honesty grows strong when leant upon; but even strong humanity, insulted and disbelieved in, may hear itself called callousness until it ceases to care for the charge.

Again, it is an absurdity that an array of certificates should be necessary for inoculating, or injecting under the skin. Such operations are almost painless, and their results are particularly valuable; so that any person who holds a license ought to be allowed to perform them without any further ado. Of all classes of experiments, they need the least safeguarding.

It is a purely annoying thing that a teacher holding an office the duties of which require that he should take out a license, should be obliged to renew it every year. No harm could follow from its being granted for the term of his incumbency, as it could always be withdrawn if abused. The Act imposes no restriction as to the length of time for which licenses shall stand good; but the Home Secretaries have hitherto made a practice of only granting them for one year.

These practical suggestions are merely the conclusions which must follow from considering the actual value of physiological experiments, the manner in which they are dealt with by the law as it is administered, and the prospects of obtaining any modification in such administration. If the whole subject were to be considered *de novo*, the field cleared of all existing legislation, and a new law passed grounded on reason and principle, I should put forward very different proposals. Then I should urge the equal claim of all sentient creatures to be protected from human cruelty, and saved from needless suffering, while admitting the superior claim of men to their use for his own advantage. And I should propose that it be a legal offence to illuse, cruelly treat, or torture, any creature whatever. This broad principle being laid down, special provision should be made for the various cases in which it was necessary or allowable to inflict pain upon animals (among which scientific experiment would be one), and the needful conditions for each should be specified. But the day of such rational and consistent law-making as this, seems very far away.

NOTE.—While these pages have been passing through the press, the "Vivisection Abolition Bill" referred to on page 99, has again been presented to Parliament. The second reading was moved by Mr. Reid, on April 4, supported by Mr. George Russell, and opposed by Mr. Cartwright, Dr. Playfair, and Sir William Harcourt. The discussion had not closed when the hour for the suspension of the debate arrived, and consequently no division was taken. This is much to be regretted, as there could be little doubt of the result. It would have shown that the common sense of the British Parliament now sees that zoophilism has had more than its fair share of influence, and that it is now the turn of philanthropy. Sir W. Harcourt took this opportunity of mentioning that it was now his practice only to allow certificates upon the recommendation of the "Association for the Advancement of Medicine by Research," a body consisting of the most eminent medical men in the kingdom.

CHAPTER IX.

CONCLUSION.

Summary of previous argument—Supposed demoralization of experimenters—Where the real danger lies—Conclusion.

LET us now bring together the conclusions to which we have been led by this inquiry, which we may accept as proved, and use as grounds of action. We shall see that we have gathered no scanty harvest of facts and reasonings.

Pain is caused by the excessive stimulation of a nerve; it can only be recognized by consciousness, and is felt keenly in a rough proportion to the mental (which is part of the nervous) development of the individual. The lower animals suffer absolutely much less than man, in varying degrees.

The infliction of pain without justification—or with insufficient justification—is cruelty. Sufficient justification consists in the attainment by such infliction of a good which more than counterbalances the evil of the pain given. Long life, activity, and health, are benefits which counterbalance pain even to the same individual; when the benefits accrue to an individual of a higher class, and the pain falls upon one of a lower, it is still more fully counterbalanced; when the benefits are to many of the former, and the pain to a few of the latter, the advantage is still further increased; and when (the other conditions continuing the same) the benefits are permanent, and the pain transient, there can remain no doubt that the justification is sufficient. Such is the case with all experiments which advance physiological knowledge. The longer life, restored health and activity, of an incalculable number of men and women, extending over a considerable time for the individual, and—for the race—over the whole period of its existence, are gained by the endurance for a short time of varying degrees of annoyance, distress, and pain, by a comparatively small number of the lower animals. There is, therefore, no cruelty in the performance of such experiments. If a physiologist makes an experiment which has no beneficial result, the act has proved in itself a cruel one, and is to be regretted; but he himself was not cruel in performing it, if he merely committed an error of judgment, and thought that it would prove useful. On the other hand, if he has been indifferent to the pain caused, and careless whether or not he gave more than was necessary—he has been cruel, and there is no defence for his conduct.

There are other moral considerations besides cruelty in this question. It is alleged that the practice of experimentation tends to harden the heart of the operator, and so demoralize him; but if the act itself be not wrong, there can be no demoralization in practising it. The mere witnessing of pain habituates the nerves to resist agitation, but does not necessarily make the heart indifferent to suffering,* as is seen every day in the case of surgeons. There is no

---

* Professor Ludwig, of Leipsic, who was recently President of the local P.C.A.S., treats his dogs with the greatest kindness : and when he is obliged to fasten them down, arranges little pads and cushions so that they may be as little uncomfortable as possible. He considers that the being tied is generally what a dog dislikes most.

moral injustice in causing one creature to suffer for the good of another; for it is one of the most fundamental of natural laws, and that out of which all the physical and moral perfections of organic nature have sprung. The absolute condition of the life of animals as the friends and servants of man, instead of as his enemies—is that he should be at liberty to apply this law to them for his own benefit, instead of leaving the struggle for existence to enforce it on them for that of their race. Among the benefits which he seeks by its application, those gained for him by physiology are some of the greatest. Consequently, no moral consideration forbids him to seek them.

The making of physiological experiments upon animals is usually—but incorrectly—called Vivisection. It forms but a small part of the work actually done in physiological laboratories in England. It is always performed (where possible) under anæsthetics, and the number of cases in which these are dispensed with is very small. There is always a distinct object for every experiment.

All true medicine is founded upon an accurate knowledge of the organs of the body, their working in health, and their derangements in disease. This cannot be obtained without experiment upon living bodies of a type generally resembling the human. The greater part of our knowledge of the most important functions of our system has been gained in this manner, and rational treatment would be impossible without it.

The practice of the healing art has been directly assisted also by experiments which have perfected treatment, tested new drugs, &c., and introduced methods of prevention as well as of cure.

Since, therefore, experiment upon living animals (with a sufficient object) is morally justifiable, and scientifically necessary, we conclude that to check it is a blunder, and to prohibit it would be a crime. It is therefore to be desired that no further steps should be taken towards abolition, and that the present law should be administered in a manner which would give greater liberty to physiologists of recognized character, while maintaining the existing safeguards against abuse of that liberty by persons of a different type.

It may be well to recur to a point upon which much stress is sometimes laid, but which has not occupied a large space in our argument. This is the effect of the practice of such experiment upon the mind of the operator.

There can scarcely be a more misleading expression than that which describes experimental physiologists "as persons whose business it is known to be to inflict on animals any amount of suffering requisite for the special purpose of benefiting men."* The business of a physiologist is to study physiology. In the course of that study, he may find himself obliged to give pain; that is a disagreeable accident of his profession, not its characteristic, still less its essence. This book has been written to very little purpose, if the reader has still to learn that the performance of painful experiments forms but a small part of the work of the investigator; and why should his whole character take its tone from one process occasionally necessary to his researches? A process, be it remembered, which we have assumed to be fully justified by his reason and conscience.

There is no doubt that the profession of a physiologist has its moral dangers; so has every other profession, or position in life. Is there no possibility that a barrister may weaken his love of truth and justice by doing his utmost for the success of his client, whether he be in the right or in the wrong? Are there no moral pitfalls in the way of the attorney? Is life in the army free from

* Mr. Hutton, in the *Nineteenth Century*, January, 1882, p. 34.

temptation, and is a commercial career the best school of honour and honesty? Is there no risk to the clergyman in his daily familiarity with the highest aspirations and the lowest vices? In fact, every profession has its special temptations, and there is no reason to suppose that physiology has more than others. Possibly, some experimental physiologists are rough and careless; so are some surgeons and dentists. Such men are probably coarse and cruel by nature, and their work—having to do with suffering—throws this fault into strong relief; but there is no proof that they *became* cruel in consequence of pursuing it. Even granting—what is certainly probable—that the necessity of inflicting pain may render some natures indifferent to it, this is no more a reason for abolishing experimental physiology than for abolishing surgery or dentistry. The risk is not so great as is believed by those who only view the matter from the outside, but at any rate it must be encountered.

It would be an endless task to go into all the work which has been done by all experimenters, and apply the rules which we have laid down to each case. Without entering upon any wholesale justification or condemnation of any man or group of men, I have attempted to trace out what experiment has been, need be, ought to be, and is in England, which is all that practically concerns us. Wherever it has been carried beyond the limits which reason and justice have marked, it is emphatically to be repudiated by all just and merciful men, but most strongly of all by those who owe allegiance to the noble profession which is thus misrepresented. It is one of the most disastrous effects of the "anti-vivisection" agitation that it has rendered this simple act a hard one, requiring a moral effort, instead of springing spontaneously from a righteous indignation. Indiscriminate attack leads to indiscriminate defence. So long as war was waged only upon the abuses of experiment, all those who recognized its uses were willing to join in the effort; but when experiment itself was attacked, and all who practised it alike condemned as cruel, they were all obliged to make common cause in its defence, regardless of the differences which had been so conspicuous before. And it is undeniable that the effect of such comradeship is not good. The real danger of "demoralization" to physiologists arises, then, not from practising their profession freely, but from being hindered and calumniated in pursuing it; and those philanthropists who are so anxious for their moral welfare would best consult it by letting them alone.

It is now clear that the total abolition of experiments on living animals would be simply disastrous to the advance of physiology, medicine, and surgery, and thus would greatly hinder the diminution of suffering—both human and animal. On the other hand, the interests both of man and beast would be furthered by a more enlightened and liberal treatment of experimenters, at present kept under police surveillance as members of "the dangerous classes." Cruelty is intolerable, and cannot be tolerated. The resolutions passed by the Physiological Section of the British Association in 1871, already referred to, are the authoritative acceptance by English physiologists of the principle that no avoidable pain should ever be inflicted upon animals. And, indeed, any other course is simply immoral.

There is only too much suffering in the world already, and the man who adds a needless grain to that terrible mountain, is a murderer *in posse*. The use of anæsthetics (where possible) follows as a matter of course. Painful experiments should never be attempted by unskilled persons; the marvellous vibrations of sentient nerves were not made to be clashed into discord by the hand of a blunderer.

And even the skilled inquirer should call for that keen response only with a sufficient and clear reason.

But, when all these limitations have been laid down, experiment will still be seen to remain absolutely necessary to certainty and security in medicine. The phenomena of the human body can be only imperfectly studied while it is living, and only the arrangement of its parts can be perfectly studied when it is dead. Thus, deductions drawn both from bedside observation and dissections, may remain vague and inconclusive, while one series of experiments upon a living animal would either confirm or disprove them.* But at the touch of experiment theory crystallizes into fact. It affords the only solid ground upon which Medical Science can stand; it alone gives Physiology a right to be called a science at all. Only of what has been tested by experience can we really say—*we know;* and every first experience is an experiment.

A striking example of the success and failure of the two opposite methods of inquiry is furnished us by Sir Charles Bell, the eminent physiologist, who lived and worked about seventy years ago. At that time, no one thought of interfering with the use of the lower animals for purposes of investigation; but the feeling against the dissection of human bodies was very strong. In his anxiety to uphold the study of human anatomy, he rather neglected and decried (by comparison) experimental work; he did in many cases what the Zoophilists now tell us that physiologists ought to do in all—endeavoured to prove his theories by anatomical deduction alone. What was the result? He spent years of his valuable life in trying to establish a natural system of nerves; it was for a time accepted, but has now proved to be not only mistaken, but useless. For want of making experiments, he wasted priceless time and labour upon a

* Appendix C., ¶ 2.

false track. But, on the other hand, in his investigations into the origin and functions of the motor and sensory nerves, he did test his theories by experiments on living animals; and this portion of his work remains as one of the keystones of Nervous Physiology, and alone renders his name illustrious. These are his own words: "These experiments satisfied me that the different roots and different columns from whence these roots arose were devoted to distinct offices, and that the notions drawn from Anatomy were correct."*

Now that we have learnt something of what Physiology owes to experiment, we can see more clearly what she would be without it,—a vague and hazy pseudo-science, working by guess, rashly trying by-paths in the dark, or timidly standing still for fear of making a mistake, blundering about among human lives, taking up a theory to-day and dropping it to-morrow, nebulous, inconsequent, untrustworthy. We can hardly realize the picture, because we have never seen her so. Hitherto she has advanced, like other true sciences, hand-in-hand with experiment and observation,—sometimes slowly, it is true, and sometimes making mistakes; but always advancing, and always gaining increased power to cure sickness and soothe pain, and also to lessen or prevent the sufferings of those very classes of animals by whose means so much has been learnt. Is it Physiological Cruelty to help this advance, or to check it?

Nothing now remains to add, except to commend this difficult subject to the dispassionate consideration of all who can place Truth above Feeling, still more—above Prejudice; who can put aside the attraction of desire, and the yet stronger attraction of abhorrence, in order to see,

* *An Exposition of the Natural System of the Nerves of the Human Body*, &c. By Charles Bell, &c. Spottiswoode, 1824, p. 31.

not what they wish to see, or what they dread to see, but what *is*; and whose real benevolence can heartily rejoice—with no *arrière pensée* of disappointment—when a fascinating horror, seen by the torchlight of excited imagination, fades in the daylight of fact into one of the many disagreeable—but not particularly appalling—duties of life. Such persons will scarcely need to be once more reminded that it is no true humanity which is willing to perpetuate a great mass of obscure misery, out of sight and out of mind, in order to spare itself the recollection of a few cases of suffering, the details of which it exaggerates and dwells upon with an ignorant and morbid sensationalism. Nor will they be at any loss to answer the question: Where and what is Physiological Cruelty?

APPENDIX A.

POPULAR FALLACIES ABOUT EXPERIMENT.

It cannot be denied that our present legislation with regard to experiment is in a much greater measure the result of an excited state of popular feeling than of the evidence laid before the Royal Commission and Parliament. It seems therefore desirable to show that this state of feeling was at the time known by competent judges to be exaggerated; and that many of the ideas about "Vivisection" on which it was founded and by which it has been maintained are simply fallacious.

¶ 1. In a letter addressed, by command of Her Most Gracious Majesty the Queen, to the President of the Royal Society for the Prevention of Cruelty to Animals, by Lieutenant-General Sir T. M. Biddulph, K.C.B., the following sentence occurs, which shows that Her Majesty's kind heart has been needlessly pained by the unfounded assertions that have appeared in print :—"The Queen hears and reads with horror of the sufferings which the brute creation often undergo from the thoughtlessness of the ignorant, and she fears also sometimes from experiments in the pursuit of science."

Should this little work ever be honoured by the perusal of Her Most Gracious Majesty, it is earnestly hoped that it will have the effect of dispelling her fears, and convincing her that no class of her subjects are more anxious to prevent the sufferings of animals than those who perform experiments upon them, and that her suggestion as to the use of anæsthetics had been anticipated.

¶ 2. The ROYAL COMMISSION appointed in 1875 "to inquire into the practice of subjecting live animals to experiments for scientific purposes," recognized the errors brought about by hearsay evidence. On page ix. the Report says :—"Much allowance must be made for the misunderstanding and exaggeration to which reports on such a subject are necessarily liable when not critically examined and not based upon the evidence of eye-witnesses."

¶ 3. The able SECRETARY OF THE ROYAL SOCIETY FOR THE PREVENTION OF CRUELTY TO ANIMALS, who has always been so earnest an opponent of cruelty of all kinds, says in the work published under the auspices of the Society ("Vivisection," page 11)—"Again, a random accusation to the effect that Vivisection is Vivisection, and its practice attended with as much pain whenever and wherever and by whomsoever conducted, all difference in the methods used by operators notwithstanding, and that English physiologists are equally cruel in their operations on animals as foreign experimenters, has been made admittedly without proof, and certainly against the common experience of persons acquainted with the facts. Again, descriptions of experiments, of implements of experiments, of conduct and conversations of experimenters in laboratories, have been published in papers in reference to the present agitation in England, conveying impressions that such matters relate to English vivisections. Exposures of cruelty are valuable provided they do not mislead. It is not always convenient to identify; but, in a discussion on English practices, it is incumbent on a writer to exonerate English physiologists when narrating particular and definite circumstances in which he knows they are not blameable, while certain foreign physiologists are, instead of leaving them under the stigma of his terrible recital. Such omissions may serve a temporary purpose, but when discovered, like actual misstatements, they lead to unfavourable conclusions."

¶ 4. SIR GEORGE BURROWS, one of the most respected fathers of the medical profession, who cannot be said to have any bias in favour of vivisection, says, in his evidence before the Royal Commission : "I do think, from the conversations I have had—not with scientific people, but with humane people whose feelings are very acute, and who are horrified at the idea of cruelty being practised on dumb animals—that they have an idea that the practice of what is called vivisection is carried out to a much greater extent than it really is; and I believe that many of those persons (who are persons of strong feelings, and very humane in their nature) are under an impression that vivisection means the dissection of living animals; they think that these operations upon the living body are somewhat analogous to that of dissection on the dead body. I am sure that there is a confusion in their minds on the subject, and it ought to be made well known to the public that really what is called vivisection very often is something so trifling that, as your Lordship put it to me just now, you would never think of employing an anæsthetic to perform it ; and also experiments that are performed on animals very often do not imply any cutting at all ; no instrument is used ; you have to administer a medicine or a poison to see what the effects are. Now we know pretty well what the effects of strychnine on an animal are ; but an experiment might be performed to show the effects of strychnine on the nervous system or the muscular system, and there is no cutting. So also an experiment might be performed to see the effect of inoculation ; you might inoculate an animal ; if you inoculated a human being to prevent some particular disease, you would hardly call that vivisection." (Question 155.)

¶ 5. One of the members of the Royal Commission seems to have shared the popular view concerning the meaning of the word vivisection, since in one question (No. 3592) he asked, "Have you cut up any dogs or cats by vivisection ?"

¶ 6. Ideas almost incredibly wide of the truth seem to be present in LORD COLERIDGE'S mind concerning physiological experiments. He says (*Fortnightly Review*, Feb. 1882) :—" Suppose it capable of proof that by putting to death with hideous torment 3,000 horses you could find out the real nature of some feverish symptom, I should say without the least hesitation that it would be unlawful to torture the 3,000 horses." Such a thing never has been done, nor is it in the least degree likely ever to be done ; but Lord Coleridge would hardly have thought the case worth putting if he had known it to be absurd, and it therefore fairly measures his acquaintance with the subject.

¶ 7. In some people's minds the cruelty of wanton young men and boys has been confounded with experiment for scientific purposes, and there are some who actually believe that students of medicine cut up live animals. Upon this point the following passages occur in the Memorandum published in 1882 by the ASSOCIATION FOR THE ADVANCEMENT OF MEDICINE BY RESEARCH, an association consisting of the leaders of the medical profession :—

"It has been imagined that students of medicine perform operations upon living animals, in order to gain manual dexterity : such a practice would be as useless as it would be reprehensible, and has never, we believe, been thought of. For our veterinary surgeons it would be quite unnecessary, and they have always reprobated the practice.

"It has also been supposed that students might, for amusement, perform physiological experiments upon living animals. This would be practically impossible, since not only are knowledge and skil necessary, but a properly equipped laboratory and suitable appliances. If, however, any ill-disposed person without scientific object or training should be guilty of cruelty most alien from the practice and the training of the profession, there is no doubt that every member of it, teacher, or student, would help to detect and punish such conduct. The case has never arisen; if it did, it could be efficiently dealt with under the law known as 'Martin's Act.'"

¶ 8. These statements are fully borne out by the Report of the ROYAL COMMISSION and the evidence elicited by them from the teachers. Referring to this point, they say in their Report (p. xvii.): "So far as our evidence goes, such cases appear to have been exceptional and abnormal." .   .   .   .

In his answers to questions 2034 and 2062 DR. PAVY states: "No class of students, if I know anything about medical students, would tolerate the introduction of a living animal into the theatre, and a vivisection performed on that animal, whilst the animal was not under the influence of some anæsthetic. .   .   .   .
At the commencement of my course, I am almost obliged to give a little apology for saying that the course will be an experimental one. I see upon the faces of the students sitting before me a feeling which leads me to consider it necessary to make some explanation, and to tell them at once that no experiment will be introduced which will wound the feelings of the most sensitive amongst them."

The following statement is made by DR. BURDON-SANDERSON in his answer to question 2613:—" I have had a great deal to do with students at different periods of my life, and have now a great deal to do with them, and I must say that I have never met with any tendency on the part of students to make experiments."

DR. PURSER, Professor of Physiology in Trinity College, Dublin, says in reply to question 4884:—" I think there is an impression abroad that medical students are very fond of performing experiments on animals, and that performing experiments on living animals is a very amusing occupation, and a thing which not only all students but all doctors also are very anxious to do. Now my experience is quite the reverse of that; my experience is that as a rule students have no taste whatsoever for such pursuits. The operations are extremely disagreeable to perform, extremely difficult, and extremely expensive; and I think that all those reasons would make students not take to them. Besides that, I think students would not care to perform operations which they did not think themselves competent to perform, and which they did not think that some good would come from; and I am sure that any student in our schools thinking of performing experiments would come to the professor and take his advice and get his assistance, and, if the professor thought it necessary, do it under his supervision." And similar evidence is given by many other teachers.

In answer to question 1550, the SECRETARY TO THE SOCIETY FOR THE PREVENTION OF CRUELTY TO ANIMALS, says:—"With regard to London,

I have enquired at every school, and I have not found a single place where experiments are actually performed before students. The animal is operated on in the laboratory, and brought out thence in a narcotized condition, and then it is examined by the students."

It has been urged that the mere witnessing of experiments must be injurious to the medical student's character. No evidence in support of the statement has been given, and it is not believed by the Royal Commission, for on p. 10 of the REPORT we find the following :—

"But the tendency to demoralization is connected, as the shadow with the substance, with the rightness or wrongness of the thing itself, and the evidence we have quoted above seems to show conclusively that at the medical schools where such demonstrations are exhibited under anæsthetics, the sense of humanity in the students is not in fact impaired." Report of Royal Commission, page xviii.

"Dr. Rutherford told us, speaking of the students at Edinburgh, that if an animal has been suffered to come out from anæsthesia, the students at once resent it."

"Dr. McDonnell, speaking of the students in Dublin, says, that unless he was able to give some good reason for doing away with the anæsthetics, the students would not tolerate the occurrence ; the public opinion of the students would be strongly against it."

After a careful consideration of the entire subject, the Royal Commissioner concluded :—"That the abuse of the practice by inhuman or unskilful persons,—in short, the infliction upon animals of unnecessary pain—is justly abhorrent to the moral sense of your Majesty's subjects generally, not least so of the most distinguished physiologists, and the most eminent surgeons and physicians."

¶ 9. A most independent proof of the fact that scientific men are as anxious as others to prevent the unnecessary infliction of pain for the ends of science* is afforded by the following resolutions passed by the PHYSIOLOGICAL SECTION OF THE BRITISH ASSOCIATION so long ago as 1871, even before popular feeling was excited in the matter.

1. "No experiment which can be performed under the influence of an anæsthetic ought to be done without it.

2. "No painful experiment is justifiable for the mere purpose of

---

* The following quotation from a Manual of Physiological Experiment by a well-known Continental physiologist, will serve to show that humane consideration for animals is not confined to this country: "An experiment involving vivisection should never be performed, especially for purposes of demonstration, without previous consideration whether its object may not be otherwise attained;" and, as a second rule, "insensibility by chloroform or other drugs should be produced whenever the nature of the experiment does not render this absolutely impossible."—Cyon, *Physiologische Methodik*, p. 9.

[Note on page 7 of Memorandum of Association for the Advancement of Medicine by Research.]

illustrating a law or fact already demonstrated : in other words, experimentation without the employment of anæsthetics is not a fitting exhibition for teaching purposes.

3. "Whenever, for the investigation of new truth, it is necessary to make a painful experiment, every effort should be made to ensure success, in order that the sufferings inflicted may not be wasted. For this reason, no painful experiment ought to be performed by an unskilled person, with insufficient instruments and assistance, or in places not suitable to the purpose.

5. "In the scientific preparation for veterinary practice, operations ought not to be performed upon living animals for the mere purpose of obtaining greater operative dexterity."

¶ 10. In a memorandum drawn up by sixteen of the leading TEACHERS OF PHYSIOLOGY in England, Scotland, and Ireland, before the passing of the Act in 1875, the following protest occurs :—

"We repeat the statement which most of us have made before the Commission, that within our personal knowledge, the abuses in connection with scientific investigation against which in this Bill it is proposed to legislate, do not exist, and never have existed in this country."

¶ 11. Another favourite fallacy is that the practice of performing experiments upon living animals brutalizes the operators, and renders them callous to the sufferings that they inflict; but of this there is no evidence, and the well-known characters of some famous experimenters are proof to the contrary.

Haller, the father of experimental physiology, was equally renowned for his piety, gentleness, and humanity. Harvey, Sir Charles Bell, and many others, express deep regret at being obliged to operate upon living animals. So far from becoming hardened in the course of their work, the tendency among physiologists seems to be in the opposite direction, towards increased sensitiveness and sympathy. Sir William Fergusson, speaking to the Royal Commission of Mr. Syme, said (Question 1028): "He lived to express an abhorrence of such operations, at all events if they were not useful ;" and also remarks : "I would not perform some of the operations at this present time that I performed myself in earlier days." Many physiologists have renounced the practice on account of the pain it caused them. With the improved methods, and the abundant anæsthetics of the present day, this deterrent cause is not as strong as it was ; but the fact remains that long practice was far from hardening the nerves even of noted operators. And it must be observed that the capital which has been (often untruly) made out of the repentance of vivisectors is inconsistent with the argument that the practice is brutalizing.

Mr. Jonathan Hutchinson well says : "There have been perhaps few circumstances brought to light in the recent discussion on the subject of vivisection more humiliating than the ease with which a certain section of the public can conceive it possible that the performance of painful experiments may have in it an element of attractiveness to the operator. It might have been expected that those who for the first time learned that such things were occasionally done would, judging from their own sentiments, have at once felt it to be impossible that any should undertake them, excepting under motives of compelling duty strong enough to overcome a natural repugnance of the most potent kind. What we have witnessed has been, however, somewhat different; and the revelation that there are amongst us many who believe that there must be something intrinsically pleasant in the infliction of suffering is by no means one of an encouraging character."
—*Fortnightly Review*, September, 1876, note on p. 311.

¶ 12. The "International Association for Total Suppression of Vivisection," has lately re-published the Memorandum of the "Association for the Advancement of Medicine by Research," with criticisms and answers—or what are intended as such. Most of these relate to matters already treated of in the present book, and do not call for any additional remark. One point, however, must be noticed, as it seems to be considered a strong argument. The "Memorandum" says: "It is true that there are special difficulties in the study of the natural laws of living bodies." The comment on this is : "This is true, but it has nothing to do with Vivisection. The latter is the study of *artificially-induced conditions* in living bodies—a distinct and wholly superfluous field of observation" (page 4). Therefore, we are to understand that if a man falls into a well containing carbonic oxide gas, his symptoms are the result of a natural law ; but if a dog is put into a receiver full of the same gas, his symptoms being the result of "artificially-induced conditions" constitute a "distinct field of observation," and no conclusion can be drawn from the one for the other! "Nature is made better by no mean, but Nature makes that mean," and so also with those means by which she is made worse. A condition of any kind can only be induced by the use of existing natural influences ; and when they have been brought into action, that action is just as natural, and just as subject to law, as if the circumstances had arisen spontaneously.

APPENDIX B.

AMOUNT OF SUFFERING INFLICTED.

THE following quotations from the published statements of persons who must be accepted as the best judges on the subject, show clearly that, since the introduction of anæsthetics, the amount of pain actually inflicted in experiments upon living animals is insignificant. They relate, of course, to England alone.

¶ 1. MR. CHARLES DARWIN, in his evidence given before the Royal Commission, says (Question 4670) :—"From all I can learn, the exceptions are extremely few in which an animal cannot be experimented on in a state of entire insensibility."

Mr. Darwin's known impartiality and strict accuracy give additional weight to his judgment.

SIR THOMAS WATSON said (Question 19) :—"I believe that most of the experiments may be conducted with very little expense of pain to the animal."

The REPORT itself states that:—"By the use of anæsthetics in humane and skilful hands, the pain which would otherwise be inflicted may, in the great majority of instances, be altogether prevented, and in the remaining cases greatly mitigated."

¶ 2. That anæsthetics are actually employed in the cases where their use is possible appears from the following extract from the evidence of MR. COLAM, Secretary to the Society for the Prevention of Cruelty to Animals :—

"1543. In the cases in which it would have been possible, so far as time or the object was concerned, do you consider that anæsthetics have been used always ?

"I believe that generally the English physiologists have used anæsthetics where they think they can do so with safety to the experiment.

"1544. Then may the Commission take your belief to be that there is a desire on the part of the scientific men in this country so far to get rid of the infliction of pain as is compatible with the scientific object which they have in view?

"I should say so generally, but in some cases there appeared to be some heedlessness with regard to the suffering of the animal: for instance, in some of Brown-Séquard's experiments, when animals were kept for weeks in suffering.*

"1545. May I take it to be your view that the general tendency of the English scientific world is not at variance with humanity?

"I believe it is very different indeed from the practice of foreign physiologists.

"1546. So that you would treat cases of wilful cruelty, if they exist at all in this country, as exceptional cases, rather than as fairly chargeable upon any want of proper sentiment on the part of the profession?

"Undoubtedly with regard to wanton cruelty. I do not know that I know of a single case of wanton cruelty, by which I mean suffering caused without any object, except to gratify a cruel mind.

"1547. Then you give the scientific men of this country credit for using anæsthetics, and dealing tenderly with animals so far as is compatible with the objects which they have in view?

"Yes, I think so, speaking generally. As regards tenderness I have no evidence to prove that they are tender to animals.

"1548. That the cases where that is not so are exceptional cases, and not cases fairly chargeable to the profession generally?

"I think so."

¶ 3. The following extract from the Memorandum published by the ASSOCIATION FOR THE ADVANCEMENT OF MEDICINE BY RESEARCH further illustrates the feeling of the profession on this point:—"But speaking of this country, and of modern times, it may safely be said that no charge of wanton, needless, or excessive sacrifice of animals can be, or indeed has been, seriously alleged against the small number of experimental physiologists and pathologists at work in the three kingdoms. Science has herself provided the means by which pain is reduced to a minimum. The beneficent discovery of anæsthetics is one cause of the great difference between the sufferings inflicted by Harvey, Boyle, Hales, Haller, Hunter, Magendie, and Bell, and the generally painless experiments of a modern laboratory." (p. 5 et seq.)

---

* M. Brown-Séquard is a distinguished French physiologist.

APPENDIX B. 121

¶ 4 The most conclusive evidence is that laid before Parliament by the Home Office in the form of the following REPORTS :—

ENGLAND AND SCOTLAND.

32, Harley-street, W., 30 January, 1879.

SIR,—In accordance with the instructions contained in Mr. Liddell's letter of the 19th December, 1878, I have the honour to submit the following Report upon—

I. The Total Number of Experiments performed during the Year 1878, under the Act 39 & 40 Vict. c. 77.
II. The Number of Experiments, with the Names of those who do not object to the Publication of their Names.
III. I have endeavoured, as far as is possible, to determine the number of Experiments in which there is reason to believe that Pain or Suffering of an appreciable kind was inflicted.

REPORT.

1. The total number of licenses in force during any part of the year 1878, was 45 ; but as, of these, it would seem that 18 were not acted upon, the number of licensees who need be specified is reduced to 27, a list of whom is subjoined ; together with a list of those licensees who do not appear to have performed any experiments.

2. The total number of experiments performed under these 27 licenses and the certificates, according to the returns I have received from each licensee, was about 481.

3. Of these, 317 were performed under the restrictions of the license alone ; 87 under certificates specified in Column 2 ; 30 under certificates in Column 3 ; and 47 under certificates in Column 1 ; five of the licensees also held certificates in form specified in Column 4, one of whom held two such certificates ; the experiments (about 18 in number) under these certificates are included in the number of those placed under the head of certificates in Column 2.

4. As regards the *painful* or *painless* nature of the experiments, it is necessary to refer only to those which were performed under certificates in Columns 2 and 3, the former of which allows the use of anæsthetics to be dispensed with where their administration would render the experiment valueless ; and the other permitting the animal to survive the state of anæsthesia in cases where otherwise the object of the experiment would be frustrated.

5. With respect to the experiments under certificates in Column 2, it would appear from the descriptions of them with which I have been

furnished, and also in part from what I have myself witnessed, that in the majority of cases the only actually painful part of the proceeding was done under anæsthesia, an anæsthetic being administered whenever it was admissible.

Upon full consideration of all these experiments, and the mode in which they were performed, I am of opinion that the extreme number of cases in which an amount of suffering worth notice was inflicted could not have exceeded 40. I would state, however, that in 24 of these cases the animals did not suffer from the actual experiments, but, as in the experiments instituted for the investigation of certain epizootic diseases, from the after consequences only. In 16 cases alone, so far as I am able to judge, and these were confined to two sets of experiments, is there reason to believe that any considerable amount of suffering was directly inflicted.

6. As regards the experiments under certificates in Column 3, it is less easy to form a correct estimate of the actual amount of pain that may have been caused. Taking, however, all the circumstances connected with them into consideration, I believe that the amount of suffering, where any at all was inflicted, must have been very slight, in the majority of cases not being greater probably than that which necessarily attends the presence and the healing of a wound of the integument.

7. In the remaining experiments, inasmuch as they were all performed either whilst the animal was in a state of insensibility from the previous exhibition of an anæsthetic, or were experiments regarding the action of agents in themselves having narcotic or anæsthetic properties, there is no reason to suppose, from any particulars that have come to my knowledge, that any appreciable pain was inflicted. As a matter of fact, moreover, I would beg to observe that of the experiments performed under the license alone, at least 200 appear scarcely to come within the scope of the Act at all, and might probably have been performed independently of it, as not being calculated to give pain; but as they were performed under the license, they are included in this Return.

8. The number of experiments or demonstrations of physiological facts, performed under certificates in Column 1, is 47. This number distributed amongst 11 Physiological Schools, gives an average of less than five for the instruction of each class, although the discretion of the teachers is unlimited as to the number of such demonstrations they may consider necessary.

I have the honour to be, Sir,
Your obedient Servant,

The Right Honourable the Secretary of State.   GEO. BUSK.

APPENDIX B.

IRELAND.

Claremont House, Dublin, 19 March, 1879.

SIR,—In compliance with the instructions contained in your letter of the 8th instant, I beg to submit, for the consideration of his Grace the Lord Lieutenant, the following Report upon—
  I. The Total Number of Experiments performed in Ireland during the year 1878, under the Act 39 & 40 Vict. c. 77.
  II. The number of Experimenters, and the Names of those who do not object to their Publication.

REPORT.

1. The total number of licenses in force during any part of the year 1878 was 10; in five instances the license was not acted upon; the number of experimenters was consequently reduced to five.
2. The total number of experiments under the five licenses amounted to 24.
3. Of the 24 experiments performed, four were under the restrictions of the license alone, and the remaining 20 under Certificate C., Column 1.
4. From the returns received from the several experimenters it would appear that in no case has pain been inflicted, and that some of the experiments might have been legally performed without the license under the Act.

I have the honour to be,
Your obedient Servant,
W. M. BURKE.

To the Right Hon. the Chief Secretary,
  Dublin Castle.

ENGLAND AND SCOTLAND.

32, Harley-street, W., February, 1880.

SIR,—In accordance with your instructions, I have the honour to submit the following Report upon—
  I. The names of all persons who held Licenses and Certificates under the Act 39 and 40 Vict. c. 77, during any part of the Year 1879, together with the Registered Places at which the Experiments were performed.
  II. The Total Number of Experiments performed under the Provisions of the Act during the same period, and
  III. The Number of Experiments in which there is reason to believe that any appreciable suffering was caused.

Report.

1. The names of the licensees are given in the two subjoined Tables, in one of which are entered the names of those who performed any experiments; and, on the second, the names of those who performed none.

2. The total number of experiments performed under the licenses and certificates was about 270. Of these, 126 were performed under the restrictions of the license alone; 61 under certificates in Column 1; 35 under those in Column 2; and 24 under those in Column 3. No experiments were performed under any other certificate.

3. The number of experiments in which there is reason to believe that any material suffering was caused appears from the statements I have received from the operators themselves, and from my own consideration of the nature and probable effect, as regards the production of pain, of the experiments under the certificates in Columns 2 and 3, to have been about 25.

Of these, 15 were cases in which disease followed the inoculation of infectious matter, but in which no painful operation was performed; and 10 were experiments upon as many frogs, in which an incision of the skin was required for the introduction beneath it of a medicinal substance.

In none of the other experiments under these certificates, as I am assured by the experimenters, was any appreciable suffering inflicted.

4. As in all other experiments, except those done under the above certificates, the whole proceeding is conducted whilst the animal is in an unconscious condition, no pain is inflicted if the provisions of the Act are duly observed, and this there is no reason to suppose was not in all cases carefully attended to.

I have the honour to be, Sir,
Your obedient Servant,
GEO. BUSK.

The Right Honourable the Secretary of State.

IRELAND.

16, Harcourt-street, Dublin, 22 May, 1880.

SIR,—I have the honour to submit the Report desired by you, on the experiments performed on living animals in Ireland, during the year 1879, under the Act 39 and 40 Vict. c. 77.

Report.

It will be perceived, on reference to the accompanying Tables, that the total number of persons holding licenses under the Act in Ireland, during any part of the year 1879, was eight; and that only in one instance was a Certificate granted, viz., one allowing experiments on living animals, in illustration of lectures, the use of anæsthetics being obligatory.

Under the Licenses 15 experiments were performed, and under the Certificate 8, being a total of 23, all of which were free from pain.

I believe the provisions of the Act have in all cases been scrupulously observed, that no abuses in its working have taken place, and that all the experiments and observations made during the year have been of a class eminently useful to science, and calculated to lead to ends most beneficial to humanity.

I have the honour to be, Sir,
Your obedient Servant,
WM. THORNLEY STOKER.

To the Right Hon. the Chief Secretary
for Ireland.

ENGLAND AND SCOTLAND.

32, Harley-street, 18 February, 1881.

SIR,—In accordance with my instructions, I have to submit the following Report upon—

I. The Names of all Persons who held Licenses and Certificates under the Act 39 and 40 Vict. c. 77, during any part of the Year 1880, together with the Registered Places at which the experiments were performed.

II. The Total Number of Experiments performed under the Provisions of the Act for the same period, and

III. The number of Experiments in which there is reason to believe that any appreciable suffering was caused.

REPORT.

1. The names of the licensees are given in the subjoined Tables, in one of which are entered the names of those who performed any experiments ; and, in the second, the names of those who performed none.

2. The total number of experiments performed under the licenses and certificates was about 311. Of these, 174 were performed under the restrictions of the license alone ; 60 under the Certificates in Column 1 ; 79 under those in Column 2 ; 35 under those in Column 3 ; and 42 under the certificate in Column 5 ; but these latter are enumerated with those done under the license, having been performed under the same restrictions.

3. The only experiments in which there is the least reason to believe that any appreciable suffering would be caused, are among those enumerated under certificates in Columns 2 and 3.

APPENDIX B.

Under the former head the total number of experiments was 79, of which, however, 69 consisted in simple inoculation (no more painful than ordinary vaccination),* which in 38 cases was followed by no ill effect whatever. But in about 30 instances, viz., 19 guinea-pigs and 10 or 12 mice, disease appears to have ensued, which, during the brief period the animals survived, may have caused slight suffering.

In the remaining 10 experiments under this certificate, either no operation of any kind involving pain was performed, or one consisting merely in the passage of a needle through a fold of the skin in rabbits, and attended with no more pain than would be thus caused.

4. In the 35 experiments performed under certificates in Column 3, 18 also consisted in simple inoculation or the hypodermic injection of morbid secretions, with the view of tracing the development of morbific germs in the blood; and no painful effect from the proceeding appears to have been produced during the two or three days during which the animals were kept alive.

In the remaining 17 cases in which incisions through the integument were required, as those which constituted the only painful part of the proceedings were made under anæsthesia, and the animals afterwards suffered nothing beyond confinement until the wounds healed, or until killed, no appreciable suffering can be said to have been inflicted.

5. As all the other experiments, either under the license alone, or under the certificates in Column 1, were performed on animals previously rendered insensible, these experiments were necessarily painless, as there is no reason to doubt that the provisions of the Act with respect to the administration of anæsthetics, were in all cases faithfully carried out.

I have the honour to be, Sir,
Your obedient Servant,
GEO. BUSK.

The Right Honourable the Secretary of State.

¶ 5. Commenting on these reports, PROF. GERALD YEO says:—"From the figures in these reports, I have calculated that about twenty-four of every hundred of the experiments might have given pain. But of

---

* With reference to these 69 experiments, it should be stated that they consisted of two series, directed to two important objects.

One set of experiments, 29 in number, and undertaken at the instance of the Royal Agricultural Society, were devoted to the investigation of the nature and prophylactic treatment of the disease termed "Anthrax," or "Splenic fever" of cattle and sheep.

The other series (40 in number) were undertaken at the direct request of the Medical Department of the Local Government Board, and were directed to the elucidation of an obscure and fatal disease, affecting more especially persons engaged in wool sorting, and now found to be identical in nature with "Anthrax."

The results of these inquiries have been most important, and cannot fail to prove highly beneficial, both to man and domestic animals.

APPENDIX B. 127

those twenty-four, four-fifths are like vaccination or the hypodermic injection of morphia, the pain of which is of no great moment. In about one-seventh of the cases, the animal only suffered from the healing of a wound, having been completely under chloroform when the incision was made; and in about one-twentieth of the twenty-four, pain equal to that accompanying an ordinary surgical operation on the human body is inflicted. In other words, we learn from the reports that in one hundred vivisections we should find the following numbers, arranged to show the amount of pain inflicted :—

Absolutely painless	... 75
As painful as vaccination	... 20
,, ,, the healing of a wound	... 4
,, ,, a surgical operation	... 1
	100

Pain forms then but a rare incident in the work of a practical physiologist in England; and when it is necessary that any be inflicted, every precaution is used to reduce it to a minimum."—*Fortnightly Review*, March, 1882.

ENGLAND AND SCOTLAND.

SIR,—I have the honour to submit the following Report, embracing—

I. The Names of all Persons who held Licenses and Certificates under the Act 39 & 40 Vict. c. 77, during any part of the year 1881, with a statement of the Registered Places for which the Licenses were valid.

II. The Total Number of Experiments performed under the Act for the same period, and—

III. The Number of Experiments in which there was any reason to believe that appreciable Suffering was caused.

REPORT.

1. The names of the 38 persons who held licenses are given in the subjoined Tables, in one of which are entered the names of those licensees who performed any experiments; and in the other, the names of those who performed none.

2. The total number of experiments performed during the year under the licenses and various certificates was about 270. Of these, 59 were performed under the restrictions of the license alone; 90 under certificates in Column 1; 29 under certificates in Column 2; 92 under those in Column 3; and 1 under the certificate in Column 4.

3. The only experiments in which it is likely that any appreciable

suffering would be caused, are amongst those performed under the certificates in Columns 2, 3, and 4.

(a). In all the experiments under the first and third of these heads the only operation consisted either in simple inoculation with a morbid virus, or in its introduction by hypodermic injection; the proceeding in either case being no more painful than the prick of a lancet or needle.

(b). Of the experiments under the second head, 68 also consisted in simple inoculation with a morbid virus, or the introduction by hypodermic injection of various substances of a poisonous or medicinal character.

(c). In most of the inoculation experiments no effect was apparently produced, whilst in those in which the inoculation took effect, either death speedily ensued or the animal was killed after a very brief interval.

This was the result in about 20 or 25 cases, amongst which are included eight (seven mice and one frog), caused by poison in the prosecution of a recent criminal investigation.

4. In the other experiments of different kinds performed under the certificates in Column 3, the only pain caused would be that attending the healing of the wound and the necessary confinement, or in some cases produced by the action of drugs administered. The number of cases in which trifling suffering of this kind was caused might be 10 or 12.

5. As in the experiments performed under the license alone, or under certificates in Column 1, the animals are placed and kept in a state of anæsthesia, no pain need be inflicted; and I have every reason to be assured as regards the due administration of anæsthetics that the provisions of the Act are fully carried out.

Of this I have on several occasions had an opportunity of satisfying myself from personal observation in my visits to the registered places.

It may, therefore, be confidently stated that during the past year no case has arisen in which it was found necessary to inflict pain, except of the most trivial nature, in the prosecution of scientific inquiry.

I have the honour to be,
Sir,
Your obedient Servant,
GEO. BUSK.

The Right Honourable the Secretary of State.

The Report for the year 1882 has not yet been published, but there is no reason to suppose that it differs in its character from those of the four preceding years.

# APPENDIX C.

NECESSITY OF EXPERIMENTAL RESEARCH, FOR THE WELFARE OF MAN AND OF THE LOWER ANIMALS.

The Evidence proving not only the utility but the absolute necessity of making experiments on living animals is so voluminous that the only difficulty is in selection. Out of a great mass of material, it may suffice to give the following extracts, beginning with the Report of the ROYAL COMMISSIONERS, whose conclusions, drawn from the mass of evidence laid before them, must necessarily carry great weight.

SECTION I.—UTILITY TO MAN.

¶ 1. "It would require a voluminous treatise to exhibit in a consecutive statement the benefits that medicine and surgery have derived from these discoveries. Let us take for our example the discovery of the circulation of the blood, and the various improvements in the treatment of diseases, and in the safe method of performing surgical operations on the human subject, that have resulted from it. In medicine it is obvious that a knowledge of the nature of—and of the proper treatment to apply in—the large and important class of diseases of the heart and blood-vessels, could not have been acquired without a knowledge of the mechanism of the circulation. In surgery this discovery has exercised a still more direct influence; and the narrative of the improvements in practice directly referable to it would lead us by gradual and successive stages from the time when, after an amputation, red-hot irons were applied to staunch the bleeding vessels, to the employment of the carbolised ligature of the present day. If Harvey's experiments, and those upon the lacteal system, were to be performed now, the animals would first be rendered insensible to pain; and even in the case of Sir Charles Bell's experiments, where sensation was the immediate subject of the investigation, by far the most severe part would also be performed while the animal was in a state of complete anæsthesia."—*Royal Commission Report*, page xiii.

"The production of disease in animals has been already, and is likely to become still more, the source of knowledge prophylactic as well as therapeutic, tending in the most important degree to the prevention as well as to the mitigation and the cure of disease in the human family."—*Ib.*, page xiv.

"Important knowledge has also been acquired in respect of tuberculosis, that fatal malady which causes the loss of one-tenth of the whole number of the human family who die in the United Kingdom. This knowledge may be expected to receive fresh development, and to lead, if not to the suggestion of any cure, at least to the avoidance of many of the causes which now occasion the production of the malady in the human subject. For other instances of a like nature, we must refer to the evidence. The deduction we draw from them is that, whether we look to the possibility of cure or to the probability of prevention, we cannot recommend the total prohibition of experiments of this class. It consists in subjecting a comparatively very small number of animals to diseases not generally involving severe pain—and from the observation of these diseases results are likely to be derived tending to the mitigation, or possibly even the removal of some of the severest scourges which afflict the human race."—*Ib.*, page xv.

¶ 2. PROFESSOR WM. SHARPEY quotes the following sentence from Haller, in his evidence:—"But it is not sufficient to make the dissections of the dead bodies of animals. It is necessary to incise them in the living state. There is no action in the dead body; all movement must be studied in the living animal, and the whole of physiology turns on the motions, external and internal, of the living body. Hence no progress can be made in investigating the circulation of the blood and its more recondite movements, or the respiration, or the growth of the body and the bones, the course of the chyle, or the motion of the intestines, without the sacrifice of living animals. A single experiment will sometimes refute the laborious speculation of years. Hæc crudelitas ad veram physiologiam plus contulit, quam omnes fere aliæ artes quarum conspirante opera nostra scientia convaluit."—(Question 591.)

¶ 3. In giving evidence before the Royal Commission, MR. DARWIN says : "The first thing that I would say is, that I am fully convinced that physiology can progress only by the aid of experiments on living animals. I cannot think of any one step which has been made in physiology without that aid."—(Question 4668.)

The following extracts from other sources will show the practical unanimity of professional opinion upon this point.

¶ 4. At the Sixth General Meeting of the INTERNATIONAL MEDICAL CONGRESS, held in London in 1881, when 3181 medical men were gathered from all parts of the world, the following Resolution was passed unanimously :—" That this Congress records its conviction that experiments on living animals have proved of the utmost service to medicine in the past, and are indispensable to its future progress. That, accordingly, while strongly deprecating the infliction of unnecessary pain, it is of opinion, alike in the interests of man and of animals, that it is not desirable to restrict competent persons in the performance of such experiments."—*Transactions of the International Medical Congress*, 1881, vol. I., page 101.

¶ 5. In addressing the Section of State Medicine, MR. JOHN SIMON said :—" Let me now briefly refer to the fact that during the last quarter of a century all practical medicine (curative as well as preventive) has been undergoing a process of transfiguration under the influence of laboratory experiments on living things. The progress which has been made from conditions of vagueness to conditions of exactitude has, in many respects, been greater in these twenty-five years than in the twenty-five centuries which preceded them ; and with this increase of insight, due almost entirely to scientific experiment, the practical resources of our art, for present and future good to the world, have had, or will have, commensurate increase. Especially in those parts of pathology which make the foundation of preventive medicine, scientific experiment in those years has been opening larger and larger vistas of hope ; and more and more clearly, as year succeeds year, we see that the time in which we are is fuller of practical promise than any of the ages which have preceded it. It is solely by means of experiment that we can hope so to learn the causes of disease as to become possessed of resources for preventing disease."—*British Medical Journal*, August 6, 1881, pages 220 and 221.

¶ 6. In his opening address to the Section of Materia Medica and Pharmacology, PROFESSOR FRASER said :—" It is clearly appreciated by all who are actively interested in the progress of pharmacology, that it is essentially an experimental method. This method, indeed, is as old as science itself ; and although it has been the instrument by which all true progress in medicine has been achieved, during a long period in the history of medicine it had been distorted by the importation of metaphysical phantasies, and dominated by the contending theories of the schools. From data of the most insufficient description theories were evolved of wide application ; and in no department of medical knowledge was this more strikingly manifested than in pharmacology and therapeutics.

" I have already defined pharmacology as the science of the action of remedies, and pointed out that, like every other science, it must be founded upon experiment; which from the nature of its problems must be performed upon living beings."—*British Medical Journal*, August 6, 1881.

¶ 7. At the Annual Meeting of the BRITISH MEDICAL ASSOCIATION held at Ryde in August, 1881, the following resolution was passed (with one dissenting voice) :—" That this Association desires to express its deep sense of the importance of vivisection to the advancement of Medical Science, and the belief that the further prohibition of it would be attended with serious injury to the community, by preventing investigations which are calculated to provide the better knowledge and treatment of disease in animals as well as in man."—*British Medical Journal*, August 20, 1881, p. 332.

¶ 8. In addressing the meeting on the subject of the above resolution, PROFESSOR HUMPHRY said :—"It was our duty who know the real importance of vivisection to the advancement of our profession and the welfare of the community, it was our duty in the interest less indeed of our profession than of the general welfare of the public, that we should speak out and state what we think distinctly. The first argument raised against vivisection is—What good has it done? To one who surveys the progress of medical science from its beginning, this question seems scarcely to be possible for persons to ask. Why, the truth is, that almost every advance in the knowledge of the workings of the human body has been made through vivisection. Our knowledge of the movement of the blood, our knowledge of the mode of action of the heart, and the other processes by which the circulation of the blood is effected, of the functions of the nervous system, of the functions of the brain, of the functions of the spinal cord, of every nerve which passes from the brain and spinal cord, of the influence of those nerves over every organ and structure of the body, over the heart, over the lungs, over the stomach, over the pulse, over the kidneys, over the bladder, over the skin, over the muscles, is almost entirely due to vivisection. What has been the influence of this upon medical treatment? Almost all real and great advance in medical treatment has been due to better medical knowledge, and that better medical knowledge is greatly due to the advancement of physiology. Take away the knowledge which we have received through vivisection, and conceive what a chaos would be our knowledge of the human body, and our ideas of the treatment of the diseases of the human body. You can scarcely conceive to what we should be reduced. Every man in the whole history of medicine, every man who has made real advances in the knowledge of the workings of the human body, has done it through vivisection. From Galen to Vesalius, to Harvey, to

Hunter, to Hope, and Brodie,—for this, the most practical of modern surgeons, was a vivisector; every one of these men, and they are few among the many, has made his greatest discoveries through vivisection."

¶ 9. The medical profession in America is equally unanimous on this point, as is shown by the following resolution, passed by the Medical Society of the State of New York :

"That it is the unanimous opinion of the members of this society that the unrestricted performance, by qualified medical men, of scientific experiments upon animals is essential to the maintenance and progress of the science and art of medicine."

¶ 10. SIR JAMES PAGET writes :—"Speaking generally, it is certain that there are few portions of useful medical knowledge to which experiments on animals have not contributed. The knowledge may be now familiar, so that the sources from which parts of it were derived may be forgotten ; or what was first found by experiments may now have other evidences ; or, experiments may only have made sure that which, without them, was believed; but the whole history of medicine would show that whatever useful or accurate knowledge we possess we owe some parts of it to experiments on animals.

"A clear instance of its utility may be found in the tying of arteries, whether for the cure of aneurism or for the stopping of bleeding.

"Before Hunter's time, that is, about a hundred years ago, it is certain that 95 out of 100 persons who had aneurism of the principal artery of a lower limb, died of it. A few more may have been saved by amputation above the knee, but at that time about half the patients who submitted to that operation, died. At the present time, it is as certain that of a hundred persons with the same disease less than ten die.

"In the same time there has been a great diminution in the deaths from bleeding after large operations : I remember when such bleeding might be called common; it is now very rare.

"By these improvements in surgery some hundreds of lives are annually saved in this kingdom ; lives of which it may be deemed certain that, less than a century ago, ninety per cent would have been lost. Looking back over the improvements of practical medicine and surgery during my own observation of them in nearly fifty years, I see great numbers of means effectual for the saving of lives and for the detection, prevention, or quicker remedy of diseases and physical disabilities, all obtained by means of knowledge to the acquirement or safe use of which experiments on animals have contributed."—*Nineteenth Century*, Dec., 1881, pages 925 and 927.

¶ 11. SIR WM. GULL says : "Until Dr. Marshall Hall's vivisections, at the beginning of this reign, nothing was really known of the convulsive state; but his experiments made it clear that a convulsion is a mechanical nerve process, the beginning of which may be some trifling and removeable irritation, which propagates itself along nervous lines to their centres, to issue again in various directions to the muscles and other parts, much after the manner of the electrical force telegraphed to a central office, and thence outward in different lines."—*Nineteenth Century*, March, 1882, page 465.

¶ 12. Bacon, in his "De Augmentis," Book IV., Chap. I., speaks of vivisection thus: "Of that other defect in anatomy (that it has not been practised on live bodies) what need to speak? For it is a thing hateful and inhuman, and has been justly reproved by Celsus. But yet it is no less true (as was anciently noted) that many of the more subtle passages, pores, and perforations appear not in anatomical dissections, because they are closed and latent in dead bodies, though they be open and conspicuous in live ones. Wherefore, that utility may be considered as well as humanity, the anatomy of the living subject is not to be relinquished altogether, nor referred (as it was by Celsus) to the casual practices of surgery; since it may be well discharged by the dissections of beasts alive, which, notwithstanding the dissimilitude of their parts to human, may, if judiciously performed and interpreted sufficiently, satisfy this enquiry."—(*Ogle's Harveian Oration*, 1880, Note, page 140.)

SECTION II.—UTILITY TO ANIMALS.

¶ 1. With regard to the benefits which the lower animals gain from experiments, we are given much information by Mr. FLEMING, P.R.V.C., who says: "It may be as well to state that every advance made in physiology, pharmacology, and other branches of medicine, benefits animals as well as man."

"The benefits which these experiments on living animals have yielded are already great; while prospectively the same method promises to change half the art of medicine, from a curative system, with all its difficulties and uncertainties, to a preventive or protective one, applicable no less to animals than to mankind. How much pain and sickness will the world then be spared! How much loss, embarrassment to commerce, and danger to human and animal life will then be averted!"

"The contagious and infectious disorders are those which have ever been most destructive and intractable. Some of these are special to the human race, others to one or more species of animals, while some again are widely transmissible from species to species. Many of these affecting the lower creatures can be conveyed to man, as rabies, glanders, anthrax, foot-and-mouth disease, and probably tuberculosis and diphtheria. There are also the parasitic diseases of animals,

APPENDIX C. 135

several of which may be transmitted to ourselves, as trichinosis, and those due to various kinds of worms and vegetable parasites."

. . "The agents in the transmission of contagious diseases—proved in some cases, and probably present in all—are minute organisms, which need almost the highest magnifying power of the microscope in order to examine them. They are endowed with most marvellous powers of multiplication, which enable them to act with deadly energy in a very short space of time. Their discovery as lethal agencies was only, could only be, determined by means of experiments on living animals."

. . "Inoculation had to be made to test the potency of the cultivated germs, and to ascertain to what extent their diminished energy was compatible with the existence of the inoculated creature, and with its immunity from the original disease. Experiments and control experiments, very numerous no doubt, were absolutely essential in order to arrive at conclusions, and the result has been the greatest discovery of this century."

. . "The two diseases of the lower animals in which the experimental method has hitherto led to the most complete results are anthrax and chicken-cholera."

"The value of this new method cannot be exaggerated, even if it were applicable to anthrax alone. . . . . By means of this discovery, made through experiments on living animals in the laboratory, this scourge, hitherto irrestrainable and incurable, is now completely under the control of man all over the world."

"Rabies and hydrophobia (if we may employ the two designations for one disease) are only too familiar to the public by the terror they inspire.

"Much of the knowledge we possess with regard to rabies, particularly as to its symptoms and latency, has been derived from inoculation experiments on animals."

"By experiments in pathology, disease and mortality have been vastly diminished, and continued experiments in the same direction will cause further diminution. If mankind benefits, so do animals."

"The pain of inoculation is usually no greater than that caused by the prick of a pin."—*Nineteenth Century*, March, 1882, page 470, *et seq.*

APPENDIX D.

THE FUNDAMENTAL DISCOVERIES DUE TO EXPERIMENT ON LIVING ANIMALS.

There is no foundation for the doubts which have been cast by a few writers on the actual dependence on vivisection of the great discoveries of the circulation of the blood and lymph; but as such doubts have been published to the world, and as the matter is of such great importance, it seems worth while to devote some space to making it perfectly clear, except to wilful misunderstanding.

¶ 1.—Harvey and the Circulation of the Blood.

Persons have been found to dispute the fact that experiments upon living animals played any important part in Harvey's great discovery, or even that he made any discovery at all. On the first point, Harvey's own evidence must be decisive. In addition to the passage quoted in the text (pp. 56, 57), I now give an almost word-for-word translation of two others, which distinctly show Harvey's method. He first collected his facts, making large use of experiments both upon dead and living animals; and having learnt from the latter the contractile action of the heart, the quantity of blood which it expelled, and the arrangement for its transmission, he then reasoned upon these data, and deduced from them his great discovery of the circulation of the blood. But the facts on which it rested were all drawn from experiment.

"Of the Motion of the Heart and Blood.

Chapter II.—*What the heart's motion is, from the dissection of living animals.*

First, therefore, in the hearts of all heretofore living animals, when the breast is opened and the capsule which immediately envelops the heart is dissected, one can observe that the heart is sometimes moved, at others is at rest, and that there is a time in which it is moved, and in which it is devoid of motion. These things [are] more manifest in the hearts of the colder animals, as toads, serpents, frogs, crabs, and snails, shell-fish, prawns, and all small fish. All things become even more manifest in the hearts of the warmer animals, as the dog, the pig, if previously you shall have attentively observed how the heart commences to be moved with force, and to be moved more languidly, and as it were to fade away; for then you will be able distinctly and clearly to trace the pauses of the motion itself, becoming slower and fewer and further between, and one can look into and determine more easily both what the motion is, and in what way it takes place. In repose, the heart remains as in death, loose, flaccid, nerveless, and as it were prostrate.

"CHAPTER VIII.—*Of the amount of the blood passing through the heart from the veins into the arteries, and of the circular motion of the blood.*

Up to this, of the transfusion of the blood from the veins into the arteries, and of the ways by which it passes, and how from the beating of the heart it is transmitted and dispensed; about which things there are some who before, either induced by the authority of Galenus or Columbus or the reasons of others, say that they agree with me. Now indeed when I shall speak of the amount and propulsion of the passing blood which remain (subjects very worthy of consideration), they will appear to be so novel and unheard of that not only shall I fear some harm to myself from the envy of some, but I shall dread lest I shall make all men enemies. So much does habit, or learning [teaching] once drunk in, and deep-rooted like a second nature, sway all men, and a venerable respect for antiquity compels most men to consider things new as naught. However, now the die is cast, my hope [is] in the love of truth, and in the fairness of learned minds. Afterwards indeed, as well from the dissection of living things for the sake of experiment, and the opening of arteries, by various research, as well from the symmetry and magnitude of the ventricles of the heart and of the vessels coming into and going from [it] which nature (doing nothing without a purpose) has not made proportioned in vain to these vessels, as well from the precise and careful workmanship of the valves and fibres, and the rest of the heart's construction, as from many other things, I often and seriously would consider with myself, and the longer I would revolve it in my mind how great forsooth might be the amount of the transmitted blood, and how in a short time it is transmitted; nor however could I think that it could be supplied from the juice of food absorbed, but that we would have the veins empty and entirely exhausted, but the arteries burst by the too great influx of blood, unless the blood somehow should return again from the arteries into the veins, and come back to the right ventricle of the heart. I began to consider with myself whether it had a certain circular motion, which I afterwards found to be true, that the blood is pushed forward and propelled from the heart, through the arteries, into all parts of the body, by the pulse of the left ventricle of the heart, thence into the lungs through the arterious vein from the right; and again by the veins into the hollow vein, and thence return to the right auricle, and from the lungs by the artery called veinous to the left ventricle—as is before mentioned."

Words can be no plainer—statements cannot be more positive—than these. If Harvey discovered the circulation of the blood at all, he discovered it by reflection upon facts supplied to him by vivisection.

But did he discover it at all? It is asserted that he was anticipated by Servetus, Columbus (Realdus), and Cesalpinus. Both Servetus and Columbus had a very clear conception of the pulmonary circulation, *i.e.*, the flow of blood from the right ventricle of the heart to the lungs, and its return into the left auricle by the pulmonary artery; but they had no knowledge of the circulation through the rest of the system, and I have not even seen any distinct assertion that they had. The real dispute is as to the amount of knowledge possessed by Cesalpinus of Arezzo, for whom some Italians claim the honour which the rest of the medical world awards to Harvey.

Cesalpinus's chief treatise ("Questionum Peripateticarum, libri quinque") was published in the year 1571. In the year 1598, Harvey became a student at Padua, and probably learnt whatever was then known upon the subject from his anatomical teacher Fabricius, a man of high reputation. What he had to teach was "that the purpose of the valves in the veins was not to favour the passage of blood to the heart, but to prevent over-distension of the veins by the blood in its passage through the venous trunks to their branches, and also to retard the current of blood, so that time might be given for each part to take up its proper nutriment; and he states that valves are not required in the arteries, because, on account of the thickness and strength of their coats, they are not liable to be over-distended. Neither are valves required to retard the stream of blood, because in the arteries there is a perpetual flux and reflux of blood."* This was the best explanation that could be given by the first anatomist of Italy, more than thirty years after Cesalpinus was supposed to have discovered the circulation of the blood.

Let us now glance at some of Cesalpinus's own statements on the

---

* Dr. George Johnson, in his Harveian Oration, delivered June 24, 1882, to which I am indebted for most of the information contained in this note. The passage referred to will be found in the work of Fabricius "De Venarum Æstiolis," p. 2, published in 1603.

subject of the motion of the blood, bearing in mind that in his time, the pulmonary circulation was fairly well known, while the prevalent idea was that in the veins and arteries of the rest of the body the blood moved backwards and forwards, the fluid in the former being of a nutritive nature, that in the latter what was called *auctive*—or energizing. He says: " The vena cava and the aorta, after entering all the viscera except the heart, pass beyond them, or if any come to an end, they are resolved into *capillamenta*, and do not pour their blood into a cavity, for nowhere except in the heart is the blood contained in a cavity out of a vein."* From this passage two things are evident: firstly, that he considered the vena cava as *conveying* (instead of collecting) blood, equally with the aorta; secondly, that his *capillamenta* are not our capillaries (which moreover he could not have discovered without the microscope), because they were not vessels at all, but the supposed hair-like terminations alike of veins and arteries.

Again, Cesalpinus agrees with Aristotle that the main function of the brain is to cool the blood collected within it. "For this purpose, not a few and large, but many small veins from the aorta *and the cava* are distributed to the brain, which is supplied with blood, not gross and thick, but thin and pure."† Here we have the vena cava again conducting blood.

"A nerve," he says,‡ "is nothing more than the extremities of the aorta." But, "if the spirits are conveyed through the nerves for the purposes of sensation, it does not follow that the sentient part is of a sanguineous valve, for the nerves do not convey blood."§ Consequently no blood at all passes out at the extremities of the arteries !

" But the vena cava distributes branches throughout the whole body, in order that, together with the arteries, they may nourish every part."|| "As rivulets draw water from a fountain, so do *the veins* and arteries draw blood *from* the heart."¶ " The fountain of blood in the heart being distributed into four vessels—viz., the *vena cava*, the aorta, the pulmonary *vein*, and artery—irrigates the whole body like the four rivers proceeding out of Paradise." **

Is it necessary any further to multiply quotations, in order to show that Cesalpinus was ignorant of the facts that the blood in the arteries and in the veins flows in opposite directions, that it is transmitted from one to the other through minute vessels, and that the veins bring blood to the heart, instead of carrying it away from that organ? The only apparent evidence of any force to show that he really was acquainted with the systemic circulation consists in a kind of cento from his writings, composed by Dr. Del Vita, in which sentences from different parts of his different works are strung together,

---

* *Quæst. Per.* lib. v. p. 116 A. § *Quæst. Per.*p. 130. F.
† *Ibid.* p. 120 A. || *Ars Medica*, p. 488, ed. 1670.
‡ *Ibid.* p. 120, E. F. ¶ *Quæst. Per.* p. 116, A.
** *Ars Medica*, p. 1.

so as to form a distinct description of what the above extracts have proved him to be ignorant of. Eighteen distinct passages are used in this fashion, to compose about nine short printed lines. Upon this plan, any doctrine might be proved out of any book, and so discreditable a device only shows the weakness of the cause it was intended to support.

¶ 2.—Discovery of the Lacteals.

The discovery of the lacteals by Asellius has also been disputed, on the ground that the old anatomists of Alexandria had made a vague allusion to some such vessels. These vessels were certainly not generally recognized, or at all understood, until Asellius called attention to them. He describes his discovery in the following words :

"Having thrown back the intestines and the stomach towards the pelvis, all at once I saw a number of very fine white cords scattered over the whole mesentery, and spreading over the intestines by means of an infinite number of delicate rootlets. At first, thinking them to be nerves, I did not pause. But I soon remarked that the nerves of the intestines were quite distinct from these white threads, and ran a different course. Being struck with the novelty of this fact, I remained a moment silent, thinking to myself of the controversies, no less full of asperity than words, which were kept up by anatomists on the subject of mesenteric veins and their functions. When I came to myself, in order to satisfy myself by an experiment, I pierced one of the largest cords with a sharp scalpel. I hit the right point, and at once observed a white liquid like milk escaping from the severed vessel. At this sight I could not restrain my joy, and, with Archimedes, crying ' Eureka !' invited those present to enjoy the spectacle, which was so wonderful and unique that it struck them all with astonishment."—*Daremberg* : " Histoire de la Médecine."

But Asellius did not know the true destination of the vessels he discovered ; he thought they carried nutriment to the liver. His failure to demonstrate this theory made some anatomists altogether doubt the existence of the vessels.

In commenting upon this point, a writer in an antivivisectionist journal, says : . . . . "Vivisection had accidentally blundered upon an important discovery. Vivisection promptly recovered from its accident, and triumphantly proved the discovery a blunder. And so the ' discoverer' Aselli died—in his ignorance of the true bearing of his discovery. And twenty years later the anatomist Pecquet blew the theories of the vivisectionists to the winds, and freed science for ever from one more set of the ' errors' which experimental physiology had done its best to perpetuate."—" Physiological Fallacies, II. The Lacteals."—*Zoophilist*, June 1, 1881, p. 37.

The extraordinary incorrectness of these assertions cannot be better shown than by giving the exact words of Jean Pecquet, as quoted by Darembcrg, in his "Histoire de la Médecine":

"I had removed the heart of a dog and placed it on the table, and was thinking of nothing but counting the systoles and diastoles which the last efforts of its spirits produced, when I perceived a white substance like milk flowing from the ascending vena cava into the pericardium, at the place where the right auricle of the heart had been. I examined the white substance, and not being able to find an abscess which might, as I thought, have produced it, I opened the veins above and below the heart, and I found that this substance (which had no other taste, smell, colour, or consistence than milk or chyle such as I had seen pressed out of the lacteal veins) came from the subclavian branches, and a little beyond the jugular I found the opening where the liquid entered into the vein. I thought the mesentery might have sent this milk to this part by channels hitherto unknown, and that it was advisable not to neglect the knowledge a divine Providence had given me of a fact so useful to the practice of medicine. I placed my hand on the mesentery of the animal, which was still pretty warm, and whose lacteals were not yet exhausted. I had scarcely pressed when I could see the milk flow from the two sources I had already remarked in the subclavian. . . . . I continued the search for these vessels in a number of dogs, which I opened for this purpose. I found them all along the dorsal vertebræ lying on the spine below the aorta. They swelled below a ligature, and on relaxing the same I recognized the milk carried to the holes I had observed in the subclavian veins."

Pecquet's contributions to the subject are therefore all based upon vivisections.

APPENDIX E.

THE MEDICAL MINORITY.

The expression of an opinion by a regularly qualified medical man against the practice of experiment on living animals is so rare and unauthoritative as to be conspicuous by its insignificance. It is a question on which the profession is practically united, and cannot be relegated to the decision of ignorance as one upon which "doctors disagree."

In Appendix C. some evidence has been given of the singular unanimity of their judgment on the point. A very few dissentients, however, constitute a minority; and it may now be useful to make an attempt to estimate their number, and the value of their opinion.

¶ 1.—Evidence given before the Royal Commission.

Forty-seven skilled witnesses were examined before the Royal Commission in 1875. These were selected, either on account of their general eminence in medicine and surgery, or on account of their being working physiologists, or because they had been communicated with by some of the anti-vivisection societies. If persons of repute existed in the ranks of the medical profession willing to give adverse evidence, we may fairly suppose that they were called for on that occasion.

In reply to the question: "Are experiments necessary for original research?"—we find the following majority answering, "Yes."

Sir Thomas Watson, Bart., M.D., F.R.S., Physician in Ordinary to the Queen.

Sir George Burrows, Bart., M.D., F.R.S., President of the Royal College of Physicians.

Sir James Paget, Bart., F.R.S., President of the Royal Medical and Chirurgical Society.

Professor William Sharpey, M.D., F.R.S., LL.D.

George W. Humphry, F.R.S., Professor of Anatomy in the University of Cambridge.

Henry W. Acland, M.D., F.R.S., Professor of Medicine in the University of Oxford.

APPENDIX E.

Sir William Fergusson, Bart., F.R.S., Sergeant-Surgeon to the Queen.

Alfred S. Taylor, M.D., F.R.S., Professor of Medical Jurisprudence at Guy's Hospital.

George Rolleston, M.D., Professor of Anatomy and Physiology at Oxford.

John Simon, C.B., F.R.S., Medical Officer of the Privy Council.

Arthur de Noè Walker, M.D.

Lawson Cape, M.D.

Rev. S. Haughton, M.D., F.R.S., Professor of Physic, Dublin University.

A. H. Garrod, Prosector to the Zoological Society of London.

F. W. Pavy, M.D., F.R.S., Professor of Physiology, Guy's Hospital.

P. H. Pye-Smith, M.D., Lecturer on Physiology, Guy's Hospital.

J. Burdon Sanderson, M.D., F.R.S., Professor of Physiology, University College.

M. Foster, M.D., F.R.S., Prelector of Physiology, Trinity College, Cambridge.

John Anthony, M.D.

William Rutherford, M.D., Professor of Physiology, Edinburgh University.

William Turner, M.B., Professor of Anatomy, Edinburgh University.

J. Crichton Browne, M.D.

David Ferrier, M.D., Professor of Forensic Medicine, King's College.

George Hoggan, M.B.

G. Klein, M.D., Assistant Professor at the Laboratory of the Brown Institute.

E. A. Schäfer, M.R.C.S., Assistant Professor of Physiology, University College.

J. G. McKendrick, M.D., Professor of Physiology at Edinburgh.

J. Lister, M.B., F.R.S., Professor of Clinical Surgery, Edinburgh University.

R. McDonnell, M.D., F.R.S., Professor of Anatomy and Physiology.

T. Hayden, Professor of Anatomy and Physiology in the Catholic University of Ireland.

J. Cleland, M.D., Professor of Anatomy and Physiology at Galway.

Charles Darwin, F.R.S., &c.

Francis Sibson, M.D., F.R.S.

J. M. Purser, M.D., Professor of Medicine, Dublin University.

Wickham Legg, M.D., Professor of Anatomy, St. Bartholomew's Hospital.

A. Gamgee, M.D., F.R.S., Professor of Physiology, Owen's College, Manchester.

G. J. Allman, M.D., Professor of Natural History, Edinburgh University.
Sir William W. Gull, Bart., Physician Extraordinary to the Queen.
W. B. Carpenter, C.B., M.D., Registrar of the London University.
T. Lauder Brunton, M.D., F.R.S., Professor of Materia Medica at St. Bartholomew's Hospital.
A. J. Sinclair, M.D., Examiner at the Edinburgh College of Physicians.
P. D. Handyside, M.D., F.R.S.E., Professor of Anatomy, &c., at the Universities of Edinburgh and St. Andrew's.
Wm. Williams, Principal of the Edinburgh New Veterinary College.
Edward Crisp, M.D.
George Henry Lewes, Esq.

And the following minority answered "No":

George Macilwain, M.R.C.S., 1818 (retired from practice).
Wm. Benj. Archibald Scott, M.D. Edim. (late Surgeon Superintendent of the New Zealand and United States Emigration Service.)

¶ 2.—SUBSEQUENT LITERATURE.

A third exception to the unanimity of medical men is furnished by the author of a pamphlet which has lately been widely circulated by an Anti-Vivisectionist Society.* It proceeds from the pen of a medical practitioner; but it contradicts not only the avowed opinion of that profession, but also some of the best-established facts in physiological science.

The author was not one of the witnesses who appeared before the Royal Commission; and the evidence which the commissioners did not think it worth while to invite, or the anti-vivisectionist societies to invoke, need hardly occupy our attention, if it were not that this pamphlet has been largely read, and has obtained a considerable amount of credence among people who are unable to detect its blunders and misstatements. I shall therefore examine in detail some of its statements.

a.—PRELIMINARY INQUIRIES.

The author repudiates the possibility of coming to any just conclusion by reviewing the general improvements in medical practice which have followed closely in the steps of physiological discovery; and on the matter of improvement in the performance of surgical observations, he says: "It will not do, as has been the case in many of the arguments, to draw such a picture as that of an amputation in the 17th century and one performed last year, and say that the change is

* "On the uselessness of Vivisection upon Animals as a Method of Scientific Research." By Lawson Tait, F.R.C.S., &c.

due to vivisection. We might just as well point to the prisons of the Inquisition, and then to one of our convict establishments, and claim all the credit of the change for the fact that our judges wear wigs." I venture to maintain that it will do very well, because experiments upon animals have been one of the chief causes of the acknowledged change, whereas a Spanish prison never has been changed into an English one, so that the somewhat silly remark about judges' wigs cannot even be squeezed into a parallel. A catechism follows, to the greater part of which completely satisfactory answers have been given in the text. "The real questions are : What advances in detail are due to vivisection ?" This point has already been fully discussed, see pp. 51 to 83. "Could these advances have been made without vivisection ?" All that we know is—that for many centuries they were *not*. "If vivisection *was* necessary for elementary and primitive research, is it any longer necessary, seeing that we have such splendid and rapidly developing methods in hundreds of other directions ?" "Hundreds" is an absurd exaggeration ; but, setting that aside, so long as millions die prematurely every year, or suffer from preventable sicknesses, *all* methods of research are necessary, until we know all that is to be learnt of the nature of disease, and the means of its prevention and cure. "Have we made complete and exhaustive use of all other available methods, not open to objection ?" Have we burnt out the last of our pine-torches before turning on the electric light ? No,—I do not think we have, and I do not think we shall wait to do so either. The value of other modes of research is doubled and trebled when combined with experiments on living animals. Time presses ; Death does not wait ; life is short and precious,—the duty of the profession of healers is to do *all* in their power to lengthen and improve it. "And, finally, are the advances based upon vivisection of animals capable of being adapted conclusively for mankind, for whose benefit they are professedly made ?" This question is difficult to answer, only because it is very difficult to understand. If the results of vivisection *are* "advances," they must be for the benefit of mankind, and must be capable of being adopted *for* mankind, and adapted *to* it,—except in so far as they are intended for the benefit of the animal creation itself ; but what the author is aiming at in the phrase "adapted conclusively for mankind" is more than I can "conclusively" explain. If, however, he means to inquire whether conclusions drawn from experiments upon animals can be applied to human beings, the question has been answered in Chapter VIII.

β.—THE EVIDENCE OF DRS. ACLAND AND LAUDER BRUNTON BEFORE THE ROYAL COMMISSION.

Instead of general results the writer prefers "specific instances" and says " they must be analysed historically with great care."

His historical analysis opens with the consideration of "the alleged discovery of the circulation of the blood by Harvey," which "our insular pride" has claimed for him. . . . He then states "That he (Harvey) made any solid contribution to the facts of the case by vivisection is conclusively disproved, and this was practically admitted before the Royal Commission by such good authorities as Dr. Acland and Dr. Lauder Brunton." Where or by whom the conclusive disproof is given is not divulged; with great care therefore I turn to the proceedings of the Royal Commission, to seek for the admission of the highly respectable authorities named. And I find that neither of these gentlemen says one word on the subject, or even indirectly refers to it. I do not like to conclude that this is a deliberate mis-statement ; but, after careful perusal of the pamphlet, I believe it to be a fair sample of the "great care" expended by the author on his historical analysis.

γ.—CARBOLIC ACID.

He next proceeds categorically to contradict some of the evidence of the leaders of modern medicine and surgery, as to the advances due to experiment, and actually prints the following astounding sentence : "I have shown in my published writings that carbolic acid has done far more harm than good." At a time when the immeasurable value of the aseptic method of treating wounds is daily making itself more and more widely felt, when all the medical world rings with the fame of its discoverer, and when the use of carbolic acid has changed the whole routine of surgical practice ;—it is strange to hear this solitary voice uplifted to say, plaintively : "Perhaps it would have been better if we had never heard of it." Perhaps it would have been better also, if we had never heard of ligatures, or chloroform, or any other of such medical delusions ; but perhaps it would have been even better still— for the author's reputation—if we had never heard of the "published writings."

δ.—SIMILARITY OR DISSIMILARITY OF HUMAN AND ANIMAL PHYSIOLOGY AND PATHOLOGY.

It is extremely difficult to deal with statements in this pamphlet, because they are only capable of being contradicted ; and a writer desirous of observing the usual courtesies of discussion is perplexed to decide whether it is least offensive to suppose that the author knows the real facts, or does not know them. When, for instance, he states that he has seen the leg of a dog amputated at the hip-joint, and that "not a single vessel bled,"—it is only possible to ask : "Was it a living dog ? Who else saw it ?" When he goes on to assert that "our arteries act in ways altogether different from those seen in the lower animals," he says what could only be believed for a moment by people totally ignorant of physiology, and what proves that he is entirely careless as to whether better-informed persons suppose him to be so or not. It does not, however, require even the smallest independent knowledge of the subject to detect the fallacies in such reasoning as that which follows. "Their (the lower animals') pathology and physiology are absolutely different (from ours), as may be seen in the frequency of apoplexy and aneurism with us, and the almost complete immunity from them of all the lower animals, even in extreme old age. Hunter tried his best to induce aneurism in the lower animals, and failed. Injuries to arteries in the lower animals are repaired with the utmost certainty and readiness, but in man it is altogether different." That is to say, because animals enjoy better health, and have sounder tissues than most men possess under our highly artificial conditions of life, therefore they are differently constituted! One might as well say that the physiology of a robust ploughboy was radically different from that of a confirmed valetudinarian, because he would laugh at a blow, a scratch, or a draught, from which the other would suffer for months. Hunter tried in vain to induce aneurism in a *healthy* dog : granted, and so he might have tried in vain to induce it in a healthy man. With some persons wounds and injuries of all sorts heal rapidly and easily, with others (of a defective constitution) there is great difficulty in inducing them to heal at all. Can we therefore conclude that "their pathology *and physiology* are absolutely different"?

ε.—Ligatures.

The next remarkable statement that we meet with is a denial that experiment has added anything to our present knowledge of the best methods of tying blood-vessels, and the author sneers at the use of catgut, now universal in the instructed medical world. The fact calls for no further remark. He now says that he has himself made experiments upon living animals, concerning the tying and torsion of arteries, and found them to be futile, and uncertain and untrustworthy in their results. This is fully credible, and also requires no comment. The experimenters named in the text have, however, been more fortunate. Want of acquaintance with what had been done by others may perhaps account for this regrettable waste of the investigator's time, and of his subjects' sufferings ; since he informs us that his experiments were directed to "getting quit" of the ligature altogether, in consequence of "the fact that after a vessel was tied, one end of the ligature was cut off, and the other left hanging out of the wound," of course causing much inconvenience. "The amazing thing," he adds, "is that with all the experiments made upon animals, nobody ever thought of cutting the ligature quite short, and closing the wound over it." It seems a more amazing thing that a person who comes forward to speak with authority on the subject, as an original investigator, should not have known that Sir William Lawrence (as well as many others) had thought of it and done it years before. He writes thus : "The method I have adopted consists in tying the vessels with fine silk ligature, and cutting off the ends as close to the knot as is consistent with security. Thus the foreign matter is reduced to an insignificant quantity."* On account of the abscesses and other evil results which followed this practice, it was relinquished. It can now, however, be done with safety, using aseptic catgut,—a method that the author classes among "novelties, which speedily die out when applied to human beings." The aseptic system is certainly new, but the use of animal ligatures is neither a novelty nor likely to die out. It was introduced in 1814 by Professor Physick, of Pennsylvania, and improved by Dr. Jamieson, who states as the result of his observations and experiments upon sheep, dogs, and other animals—that a capsule will surround the ligature, or the vessel will be surrounded by an abundance of lymph, and the ligature destroyed.† Can the writer of the pamphlet be ignorant of these facts in the history of surgery, and of this fact in its present condition—that any surgeon who discards the use of catgut for deep ligatures would be held by the majority of his profession to be a barbarous practitioner?

Strangely does the evidence on the subject given by Sir James Paget —one of the greatest living authorities on surgical pathology—before the Royal Commission (Ques. 295) compare with what precedes : " The whole process of the recovery of an artery after ligature, and the means essential to its recovery, and the exact knowledge of all the process by which the artery is closed, could not have been ascertained without experiments upon animals, because it is as essential to know the whole process of the recovery as it is to know the particular manner in which the operation is to be performed. You might refer to a number of operations that were done for the ligature of arteries (some of which were done by Hunter himself and some by those who followed him) which failed, and the patients' lives were lost, simply because at that time surgeons had not ascertained the whole nature of the process for the repair of the injury done by the operation."

η.—SUBCUTANEOUS TENOTOMY.

On this point, the author remarks that he cannot find any record of Hunter's vivisectional experiments upon the surgery of tendons, "beyond the allusions to them by Drewry, Ottley, and Palmer in his life of Hunter." Had he extended his researches to the Hunterian

---

* *Medico-Chir. Trans.*, vol. vi.—Delpech, of Montpelier, was in the habit of using this method in 1813-1814. See Guthrie on Gunshot Wounds, pp. 93 and 94.

† *Medical Recorder*, No. xxxvii., January, 1827.

APPENDIX E. 149

Museum of the Royal College of Surgeons (one would have thought not an unlikely place to begin them), he would have found in Section IX. in Special Pathology, No. 594, a specimen which is thus described in the catalogue : "A longitudinal section of the *tendo Achillis* and of part of the *os calcis* of an ass. The tendon was divided transversely, and—it is believed—by subcutaneous section. Its divided extremities have retracted to a considerable distance from each other, but are united by a firm and compact substance, pale though vascular, and presenting no appearance of a fibrous texture. A similar substance is diffused among the immediately adjacent tissues.—*Hunterian.*"

The following note is appended. "In the life of John Hunter by Sir Everard Home, appended to Hunter's 'Treatise on the Blood, Inflammation, and Gun-shot Wounds,' it is stated that he ruptured his own *tendo Achillis*, which turned his attention to the mode of union of broken tendons. 'He divided the *tendo Achillis* of several dogs, by introducing a couching-needle through the skin at some distance from it, and with the edge cut through the tendon ; in this way the orifice healed up, and made it similar to a broken tendon. The dogs were killed at different periods, to show the progress of union, which was exactly similar to that of a fractured bone when there is no wound in the skin.' These experiments were performed in 1767, five years before Home began to work under Hunter ; but there is little doubt that this specimen is also the result of a subcutaneous section."

No. 595 is—"The *tendo Achillis* of a deer, which was divided transversely, and, it is believed, by subcutaneous section. Its interior is shown by a longitudinal incision. The divided extremities are not so far apart as those in the preceding specimen ; and the substance uniting them, which is of rather less diameter than the tendon, is harder, paler, and obscurely fibrous, like the tissue of a firm and well-formed cicatrix.—*Hunterian.*"

No. 596 is—"The other section of the same tendon."

The fact that these experiments failed to attract notice has nothing to do with their purpose or merit : it only causes regret that they were not followed up by others of a similar nature. As it is, our author consents to attribute the commencement of scientific tenotomy to the work of Stromeyer, and thinks that by so doing he denies the experiments upon living animals any share in its credit. He does not seem to be aware that Stromeyer's results rested upon a basis of vivisection ; since he only copied what veterinary surgeons (as the results of many experiments) had long been in the habit of doing upon horses. In a foot-note upon p. 71 of his *Operativen Orthopædik*, Stromeyer himself says : "From experiments on the reproduction of tendons instituted by Herr Günther, Vice-Director of the Veterinary College here (Magdeburg), on horses, it has been further shown that—even after considerable loss of substance, *e.g.*, removal of one inch in length of the tendon —the same (reproduction) so thoroughly takes place that in the intervening texture the silver-shining fibrillar substance re-appears. These experiments were moreover made with considerable exposure of the tendon, and the reproduction followed by means of a process of suppuration and granulation. Since, however, reproduction is much stronger in a horse than in man, the conclusions drawn from these experiments must be applied with great care." Further on (p. 90), the following note occurs: "Herr Günther has for many years performed tenotomy in cases of 'Stelzfuss" in horses, in the same manner as the Achilles tendon is now cut, with the smallest possible skin-wound. The result is constant and brilliant, and the animals become capable of doing the heaviest work. Former experiments, which both he and other veterinary surgeons made with tenotomy in an open wound, gave very unequal and generally unfavourable results. So that, in the case of the horse also, the certainty of results depends upon the tenotomy being subcutaneous."

Stromeyer hesitated at first to act upon the results of these vivisectional experiments, because he feared that human tendons were different from equine! Some fifty years ago, he had reached the point of knowledge of comparative physiology where the writer of this pamphlet now stands; but happily for his science, he passed beyond it, and learnt that the lower animals are, after all, the same "flesh and blood" as ourselves.

ι.—Transfusion of Blood.

On this point the author remarks: "We hear a great deal of cases in which patients have survived after transfusion, but we hear little or nothing of its failures." The following table of the result of 216 cases (see *Lancet*, August 5th, 1882, page 174) answers this remark, especially when it is remembered that the cases in which transfusion failed must have been lost, whether it was attempted or not, and the lives saved must be counted altogether to the credit of this operation.

Cases.	Number of Cases Treated.	Number Cured.	Per Cent. Cured.
Post-partum Hæmorrhage	108	63	58
General Hæmorrhage	75	38	50
Intestinal Hæmorrhage...	18	10	55
Carbonic Oxide Poisoning	15	6	40

Mr. Tait is mistaken in stating that André Libavius performed transfusion in 1594; he describes the process of transfusing arterial blood from one person into the veins of another, but says that the physician who performs the operation must be out of his senses ("parum sanæ mentis"), and in need of hellebore. ("Appendix necessaria syntagmatis arcanærum chymicarum." Frankfurt, 1815.) Only the numerous experiments performed upon animals have satisfied the medical profession of the value of so startling an operation, and of the best methods of performing it. The latter may be found summed up in the report on this subject presented to the Obstetrical Society of London, in November, 1879, by Mr. E. A. Schäfer, F.R.S.

Enough evidence has now been adduced to show that this publication is equally untrustworthy as to matters of fact and matters of physiology, and appears to be intended only for readers who are unacquainted with the first principles of that science.

APPENDIX F.

Legislation.

SETTING aside the question discussed in the text—whether the passing of any special statute was called for by the evidence given to the Royal Commission in 1875, or not, irrefragable arguments can be adduced to prove :—*a*. That the Act 39 and 40 Vic. c. 77, is far more stringent than any legislature recommended by the Commission; *b*. That the Act has been administered with a rigour never contemplated by Parliament, or expected by the profession of medicine; *c*. That the progress of physiology has been retarded in this country by the operation of the statute.

¶ 1.—OBJECT OF LEGISLATION RECOMMENDED BY THE ROYAL COMMISSION.

The Royal Commission recommended that a legislative control should be established, for two reasons : 1. To prevent abuse accompanying the great increase in physiological inquiry which they expected. 2. To afford an antidote to the unjust suspicions and abhorrence that had sprung up in the public mind. The report says (p. xvii.) :

"Looking at the circumstance that a great increase is to be expected in physiological inquiry, it appears to us most important that some legislative control should be established to prevent abuse extending in this direction. It is, moreover, much to be regretted that a feeling of suspicion, and even of abhorrence, should have been permitted to grow up among a large and very estimable portion of the public against those who are devoted to the improvement of medicine and to the advancement of science. Publicity is the antidote of suspicion, and we look to the reasonable superintendence of constituted authority as affording the means of reconciling in the public mind the sentiment of humanity with the desire for scientific knowledge."

That the expected increase in physiological inquiry has not taken place appears from the parliamentary reports given in Appendix B. That the antidote has had no remedial efficacy appears from the expressions made use of by the very persons in deference to whose opinion the statute was passed. At a meeting of an antivivisection society at Lord Coleridge's house, Cardinal Manning said:

"The history of the existing Act has shown that it is futile to attempt to separate the use of vivisection (if lawful use it have) from abuse." . . . "And believing, as I do, that it cannot be controlled, that we have endeavoured to control it, that we have had a most elaborate commission and report, that commission and report laid down the number of conditions under which this practice must be admitted; legislation was founded on that report, and I believe not only has that legislation been ineffectual, but that we have been entirely hoodwinked, and the law has not been carried into effect."

On the same occasion Lord Coleridge said:

"After considerable reflection on the matter, having read much that I would rather not have read, and having thought on the matter so much as I had the power, I have come to the conclusion that control it you cannot."—*Zoophilist*, July 1, 1881, pp. 54-57.

¶ 2. SCOPE OF LEGISLATION RECOMMENDED BY THE ROYAL COMMISSION.

The Commission had no intention of hampering in their investigations men of recognized character who were working at physiology. Their object was to establish a check upon the unskilful, the inhuman, and the inexperienced. They say (Report, page xvii): "Those who are least favourable to legislative interference assume, as we have seen, that interference would be directed against the skilful, the humane, and the experienced. But it is not for them that law is made, but for persons of the opposite character." . . . .

"From this prepossession (against interference) many of those whose position and character entitle them to the greatest weight are wholly free; and it has always yielded to the consideration that if there be a proved necessity for legislative interference to prevent abuse, such interference will be right, provided that the teaching of physiology and the prosecution of research by competent persons be not interfered with."—Royal Commission Report, p. xv.

Fortunately, the class of experimenters against whom the Commission wished to direct the law does not and cannot exist in this country.

But, unfortunately, the law has been passed, and put into force against competent persons, so that the prosecution of research has been materially impeded and interfered with. Here is what the physiologists themselves say on the subject after five years' experience of the Act :—

"Both licenses have been refused, and certificates have frequently been disallowed, and have only subsequently been granted or allowed, after long delay and by the help of strong pressure upon the Home Office. Moreover, some certificates have been absolutely refused, and in several cases experiments have been prevented owing to intimations that licenses or certificates would certainly not be granted if applied for.

The numbers are as follows :—

Refusal to allow certificates, Seven cases.
Injurious delay, amounting to practical refusal, Six cases.
Deterred from application, Five cases."

Memorandum adopted by the Physiological Society, 8th December, 1881.

So far as the doctors themselves are concerned, the fact that they consented to the passing of a law which they must have known to be superfluous, and might have known to be injurious, cannot but diminish our sympathy for their personal loss and annoyance; although it is fair to remember that they were deceived by the substitution of the expression "invertebrate" for "cold-blooded" animals in the final clause of the Act; the then Home Secretary failing to appreciate the enormous practical difference which the change would make in the operation of the Act. But the check put to the progress of medicine is a public loss, and it is not even compensated for by the successful exorcism of the phantom against which this legislation was aimed; so that the expectations under which the medical profession supported the Bill have been in every respect disappointed.

As to the nature of the investigations intended to be affected, the Commissioners say :

"It has been proposed to enact that the object in view shall be some immediate application of an expected discovery to some prophylactic or therapeutic end, and that any experiment made for the mere advancement of science shall be rendered unlawful. But this proposal cannot be sustained by reflection upon the actual course of human affairs. Knowledge goes before the application of knowledge, and the application of a discovery is seldom foreseen when the discovery is made. The first origin of a great discovery is often, like the germ of the natural life in an animal or a vegetable, so small as to be scarcely perceptible, and yet it may contain in it the seeds of the grandest results."—Report, page xviii.

In spite of this clear expression of opinion on the part of the very best authorities, we find when the Act is passed that this is the very first restriction imposed :—

Clause 3. "The following restrictions are imposed by this Act with respect to the performance on any living animal of an experiment calculated to give pain ; that is to say,

(1.) The experiment must be performed with a view to the advancement by new discovery of physiological knowledge or of knowledge which will be useful for saving or prolonging life or alleviating suffering."

Again, the Commissioners report :

. . . . "In the case of professional education, as at one of the medical schools, it cannot, we think, be denied that there is much force in the argument that teaching without demonstration, can scarcely be considered teaching."—Report, page xviii.

And the Act retorts :

Clause 3, par. 5.—"The experiment shall not be performed as an illustration of lectures in medical schools, hospitals, colleges, or elsewhere."

¶ 3.—MANNER IN WHICH THE ACT IS ADMINISTERED.

One of the recommendations of the Commissioners is as follows : "It may be found desirable that one of the conditions to be attached to a license should be that the experiments should be performed in some particular place ; but this is a detail which may vary with circumstances, and we think it ought not to be stereotyped by statute." —*Report*, p. xx.

Yet the following clause of the Act is administered, by general order, in the *most rigorous* manner possible :

"7. The Secretary of State may insert, as a condition of granting any license, a provision in such license that the place in which any experiment is to be performed by the licensee is to be registered in such a manner as the Secretary of State may from time to time by any general or special order direct ; provided that every place for the performance of experiments for the purpose of instruction under this Act shall be approved by the Secretary of State, and shall be registered in such a manner as he may from time to time by any general or special order direct."

Again, the Commissioners say :

"We think that the holder of a license, when he shall receive notice that the Secretary of State intends to withdraw it during the period for which it has been granted, should be at liberty to demand a public inquiry."—*Report*, p. xxi.

No such liberty is granted by the Act of 1875.

Sir William Fergusson, who has been much quoted against the value of experiment, said in his evidence (Q. 1054) :

"No, I certainly would not go that length of restraining rational men from doing that which they thought right; but I would enjoin great caution."

And yet we find that the men who are actually harassed by restraint are the professors and teachers of physiology, men in whom our great teaching establishments have complete confidence, and who have thus been obliged to meet solemnly to consider what could be done which, "without defeating the purpose of the Act to prevent wanton cruelty to animals, would render its operation less injurious to physiological and pathological science," and to consult " as to the steps most desirable to bring about these changes."—*Memorandum of the Physiological Society*, 1881.

www.ingramcontent.com/pod-product-compliance
Lightning Source LLC
Chambersburg PA
CBHW030257170426
43202CB00009B/787